Monmouth
and its
Buildings

Monmouth and its Buildings

by

Keith Kissack

Logaston Press

LOGASTON PRESS
Little Logaston Woonton Almeley
Herefordshire HR3 6QH

First published by Logaston Press 2003
Copyright © Keith Kissack 2003

ISBN 1 904396 01 1

Set in Times New Roman & Garamond by Logaston Press
and printed in Great Britain by
Cromwell Press, Trowbridge

For

Bethia and Hermione

Contents

Sources of Illustrations

The majority of the photographs have been taken by the writer, but on the few occasions they were not, they were taken, with permission, from the following sources: Monmouth Borough Archives; County Record Office; Parish Registers; Castle Museum; Monmouth Museum; J.H. Matthews, *Report on Ancient Records of Monmouth*, 1908.

Other Publications by the Author

Medieval Monmouth, Monmouth Historical Trust, 1974

Monmouth, The Making of a County Town, Phillimore, 1975

Life in the Monmouth Militia, 1778-1812, Monmouth Archaeol. Soc. 1975; *Monmouthshire Antiquary,* 1991

The River Wye, Terence Dalton, 1978

The Inns and Friendly Societies of Monmouth, (with E.T. Davies), Lithprint, 1981

The River Severn, Terence Dalton, 1982

Victorian Monmouth, Bosbury Press, 1984

Monmouth & its Buildings, Monmouth Historical Trust, 1991

Monmouth School & Monmouth, Lapridge, 1995

Haberdashers Monmouth School for Girls, Gomer Press, 1992

The Lordship, Parish & Borough of Monmouth, Lapridge, 1996

The Schools in the Priory, Monmouth Historical Trust, 1999

Home Front Monmouth (Second War), Monmouth County Council, 2000

Monmouth during the First War, (with Betty Williams) Monmouth Historical Trust, 2001

Monmouth Priory, (with David Williams & others) P.C.C., 2001

Monmouth Dates, A.D.55 to 1989, Regimental Museum

The Trivial Round, Life in Monmouth 1830-1840, Monmouth Borough Council

The Formative Years 1075-1257, Monmouth Borough Council, 1955

Acknowledgments

I am grateful to all who have allowed me to wander around their houses taking photographs and asking questions for this book which is now in its third edition. (One of the last was recently sold by Oxfam for £165.) I am especially grateful to Stephen Clarke and the Monmouth Archaeological Society, to the staff of both the Regimental and the Monmouth Museums for allowing me to use their archives, to the Town Clerk for letting me use the Borough archives, to John Foster for help and advice, and above all to Andy Johnson and Ron Shoesmith of Logaston Press for producing the book with so little trouble to the writer.

Preface

Keith Kissack is Monmouth's leading historian and his latest book continues some fifty years exploration of this ancient town. Monmouth's upstanding archaeology was an important factor when the Council for British Archaeology designated Monmouth as one of the top ten towns in Britain and this work reflects that importance. Mr. Kissack's sensitive choice of subject, combined with the charming prose which permeate all his works, makes this book worthy of a place on the shelves of everyone who loves Monmouth.

Stephen Clarke

Mrs. Syner, a gingerbread maker, was closing her shutters in Church Street one evening as the Liverpool mailcoach went through at full gallop. Her apron strings became caught in the harness of one of the leading horses and she was dragged almost to the Dixton Gate before the coachman could stop. He got down, thinking she might be dead, but Mrs. Syner rose to her feet, grabbed his whip, knocked out some of his teeth with the handle, and marched off to her shop to begin organising a petition for a by-pass to get the coaches out of Church Street.

In spite of the embankment from the Priory to the Monnow being very steep, it was decided that this was the only possible route, and ideas were encouraged. George Maddox, a local builder, suggested that a viaduct could be built which might be supported by slaughter houses which were much needed at the time (see p.35). He was given a prize of £10 and in 1834 set about the task with considerable success. He was also responsible for the façade of the opposite side of the street and the Market Hall.

Introduction

Shortly after the Battle of Hastings, the pacification of the southern Welsh border was entrusted to a cousin of the Conqueror, William FitzOsbern, Seneschal of Normandy. Created Earl of Hereford for the purpose, he quickly overran the small Welsh commote of Erging or Archenfield and, by 1068, had established at its southern tip the Castle of Monmouth. There, where Wye and Monnow meet, it guarded two river crossings connecting three widely different regions — The Forest of Dean to the east, Celtic Gwent to the south, and Archenfield to the north. Monmouth's strongest ties were with Archenfield, a cradle of Celtic Christianity which, in return for military service for the Norman invaders, was allowed to retain its Welsh customs, recorded in detail in the Domesday survey.

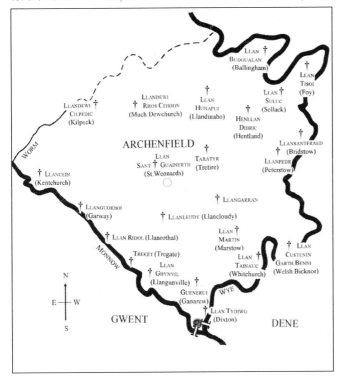

The southern extent of Archenfield

This strangely hybrid community was further distinguished when, shortly after the death of FitzOsbern in 1071, a Breton family took over the lordship and held it until 1256. One result of the Breton presence was the production of a liturgical kalendar with an accompanying collection of the lives of Welsh and Breton saints. The natural affinity between Brittany and Wales was broken when, deeply in debt to Hereford money lenders, the lordship passed to Henry III and thence to the House of Lancaster.

Earlier there had been a Roman settlement called *Blestium,* and at least two churches dedicated to Celtic saints, St. Cadoc in the town itself and St. Tydwg at Dixton on the banks of the Wye. But it was not until the beginning of the 12th century, when the timber Norman castle was being rebuilt in stone, that the rather ambiguous history of a community that was neither wholly Welsh nor entirely English really began.

Above: Herring-bone masonry in the nave of St. Peter's church (originally St. Tydwg) at Dixton. It seems to have supported a timbered wall, and may have been a rebuilding after a raid up the Wye to Hereford in 1056 during which many riverside settlements were destroyed

Introduction

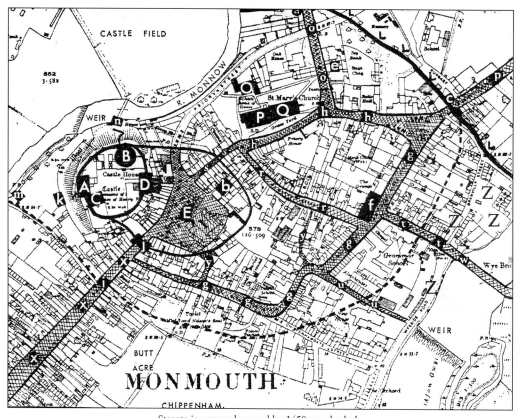

Streets in use and named by 1450 are shaded.

The Castle : A - The Great Tower
B - The Round Tower
C - The Great Hall
D - The Gate & Chapel

The Town : E - The Market Place
O, P, Q - The Priory
Z - Industrial Area (wharves etc.)

a Monk's Gate
b The Barton
c Dixton or East Gate
e Priory Infirmary
f The Grange
g Greindor (Glendower) St.
h Whitecross St.
i Gate in Town Wall

j St. Stephen's or Burnt Gate
k St. Cadoc's Church (?)
m Castle Mill
n Castle Bridge
o Monk St.
p Peter's Lane to Dixton
r St. Mary St.
s Butcher's Row
t Wyebridge St.
u Weirhead St.
v Castle Bailey St.
w Monmouth Bridge
x Monnow St.

└ └ └   Line of wall according to Leland
– – –   Possible line of Town Wall

Introduction

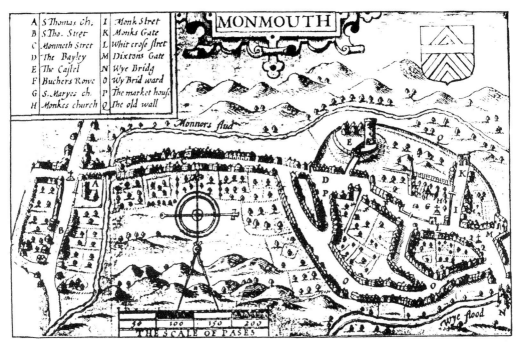

Speede's Map of Monmouth, 1610

THE MODERN
Univerſal Britiſh Traveller

An INSPECTION TABLE for this COUNTY.

MONMOUTHSHIRE, which is ſituated in the Dioceſe of LANDAFF, and Province of CANTERBURY, is

Bounded by	Extends	Contains	Sends to Parliament
Herefordſhire on the N. Gloucesterſhire Eaſt. The river Severn South. Brecknock and Glamorgan, in Wales on the Weſt.	In length, from North to South, 29 miles. In breadth from E. to W. 20 miles. And in circumference 84 miles.	6 Hundreds 127 Pariſhes 8 Market Towns	Three Members, viz. 2 for the County 1 for Monmouth.

MONMOUTHSHIRE was formerly a Part of Wales, and continued ſo till the reign of Charles II. when it was reckoned an Engliſh county, (as it has been ever ſince) becauſe the judges then began to keep the aſſizes here in the Oxford circuit.
This ſhire, as well as Monmouth, the county town, received their names from the river Monow. Uſk, which is nearer the center of the county than any other market town, is 130 miles nearly weſt from London. The principal manufacture of the county is flannel.

The *Universal British Traveller* of 1779 has a section on Monmouth and its county (opposite).

Of the town, the description includes: 'It was originally encompassed with a strong wall, some remains of which are still to be seen. The castle, of which the ruins are still visible ... [was where] Henry of Bolingbrooke, son of John of Gaunt, resided for some time ... [and] where his son Henry was born, for which reason he was called Henry of Monmouth.

The situation of the town is extremely pleasant, being at the confluence of several streams, and is both populous and well built. Besides the county hall, where the assizes are held, there is an exceeding good town-house, and one of the most handsome gothic churches in England.

In the reign of Henry I there was a convent founded here, by a Norman bishop, for black canons.

There is not much trade carried on here, except the exportation of the natural productions of the county, which are sent to Bristol by the navigation of the Wye'.

Location plan of many of the buildings mentioned in the text

1 Agincourt Square
2 The Shire Hall
3 The King's Head
4 Beaufort Court (Arms)
5 Monmouth Castle
6 Great Castle House
7 Castle & Regimental Museum
8 Castle View House
9 Priory Street
10 Slaughterhouses
11 Monmouth Museum
12 Vauxhall
13 Monmouth Priory
14 Masonic Lodge
15 Kingsley House
16 Chapel House
17 County Gaol
18 Monmouth Hospital
19 Union Workhouse
20 Monmouth School for Girls
21 North Parade House
22 Monkswell Road
23 Parade House
24 11 Monk Street
25 The Royal George
26 Oak House
27 Whitecross House
28 Baptist Cahpel
29 Working Men's Institute
30 Whitecross Street
31 Conservative Club
32 St. James's House
33 Rolls Hall
34 Cartref
35 Old Nag's Head
36 The Grange
37 Methodist Church
38 Kymin
39 Monmouth School
40 St. Mary Street
41 Duffryn House
42 Roman Catholic Church
43 The Parish Church

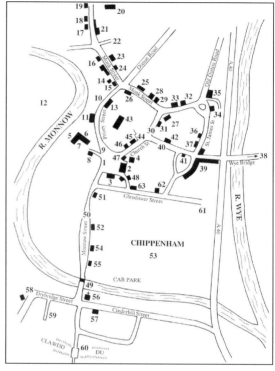

44 Church Street
45 White Swan Yard
46 Mr. Stokes, Chemist
47 1 Agincourt Square
48 Agincourt Street
49 Monnow Bridge
50 Monnow Street
51 Lloyds Bank
52 Cornwall House
53 Chippenham
54 Chippenham House
55 Robin Hood Inn
56 Overmonnow Church
57 Overmonnow House
58 Drybridge House
59 Drybridge Crescent
60 Clawwd Dy
61 Chippenhamgate Street
62 Congregational Chapel
63 Monmouth Gymnasium

THE SETTING

A town between two rivers

The view from the Hereford Road

So far, thanks to flooding, the town has been left almost completely surrounded by green fields

A town between two rivers

Top left:
The River Monnow
from Priory Street

Top right:
The River Wye from
Wye Bridge

Left:
The weir on the
Monnow at Osbaston
(the northern suburb)

THE SETTING

Flooding

Top: The Flood of 1607   Bottom: Dixton Church — The flood of 1960

Let flooding continue! The problem is never likely to be solved. Unsuccessful schemes are expensive and unsightly; 'successful' schemes would still fail to repel the floods of 1947 and 1960, but will allow speculators to litter our surrounding fields with ugly buildings.

The Kymin : The Naval Temple

The Kymin

The Kymin was first developed as a pleasure ground in 1793 when a group of 'the first gentlemen in Monmouth' decided to build on its summit a permanent pavilion or Summer House where they could hold meetings and picnics. It was a tower with ground-floor kitchen, dining room over, and flat roof above which included a telescope to view the scenery. The windows were aligned on local beauty spots, and Nelson and the Hamiltons breakfasted here. It is now known as the Round House.

The Naval temple followed in 1800, perpetuating the names of 16 admirals who had distinguished themselves during the 18th century. Nelson admired it and congratulated Monmouth on having at that time the only naval war memorial in the kingdom. The property now belongs to the National Trust.

Bridges

Possibly one of the earliest bridges was the Castle Bridge, leading from the ramparts of the castle to Castle Field, one of the town's three large open fields. The bridge was destroyed during a skirmish between local lords in 1233. It was replaced as a footbridge and then rebuilt by the landlord of the Beaufort Arms Inn, a Mr. Tibbs, in the late 18th century (top left). It led from the town to pleasure grounds which he had laid out on the banks of the Monnow. As a result the Castle Field became known as Vauxhall, and Tibb's Bridge still commemorates one of the first men to provide the amenities which were to attract visitors to Monmouth from the early days of the Wye tourists onwards.

Troy Bridge (above) carried the old road from Monmouth to Trellech, crossing the river Trothy near Troy House. In its present form it dates from the late 15th century when the nearby Manor House was acquired by Sir William Gilbert.

Wye Bridge (left) was known as Monmouth Bridge in 1282 when it was one of the boundaries of the Forest of Dean. It was rebuilt in the 17th century and three new arches were added in 1813. Just below the bridge was the weir which gave its name to Weirhead Street. Speede's map shows a similar gate to that on Monnow Bridge where Monk's Gate once stood.

Monnow Bridge replaced an earlier wooden structure in the late 13th century. The gatehouse has served as a toll-house, guard room, gaol and house of correction. In 1705 it was converted into a dwelling house 'with two good rooms on the first floor, one storey high, the other floor to garrets'. In 1819 a house which had been built against it was pulled down, the road widened, and arches for pedestrians pierced on both sides.

The Castle

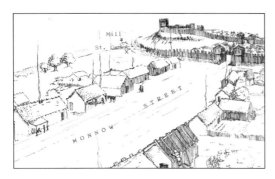

Recent excavations in Monnow Street have revealed stone age flints, Roman materials from the first century to AD 400 and much medieval pottery, whilst the Celtic church of St. Cadoc lay in Saxon times below the slope of the castle. Monnow Street is a typical market street, wide in the middle for animals and stalls, and gated at each narrow end. This reconstruction by Clive Barrett shows the pre-1100 timber castle.

The western walls of Monmouth Castle after the 12th-century rebuilding. The walls facing Wales are much thicker than those towards the town. The infilling is of early 19th-century date.

In the second half of the 14th century John of Gaunt converted the upper stages of the great tower of the castle into a more spacious and lighter habitation than that which he had inherited. Here he entertained his mother, Queen Philippa, in what was to become known as the Queen's Chamber, and here, in 1387, his grandson, the future Henry V, was born.

Above: The heads of Edward III and Queen Philippa on the great bell in St. Peter's church, Dixton

Background

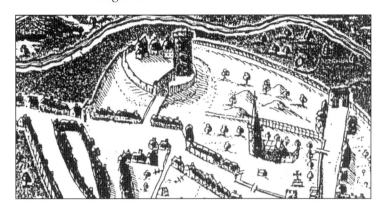

Right: The round tower at the castle from Speede's map of 1610

Below right: The remains of Monmouth Priory c.1800

When, in 1256, the lordship passed from the Breton family to Henry III, the castle had acquired a round tower, similar to the one at Skenfrith, the possessions of the priory extended into Herefordshire and Gloucestershire, and a borough organisation with its own seal (page 13) was firmly established. In 1267 the Honour of Monmouth passed to the king's second son, Edmund, on his creation as earl of Lancaster, and for the ensuing centuries, together with the three castles of Grosmont, Skenfrith and White Castle, it was an important part of the great Lancastrian estate. By the end of the century the four bridges, which the castle controlled, had been rebuilt in stone.

There is no mistaking the purpose of the Act of Union of 1536. The preamble calls it 'An Act for Laws and Justice to be ministered in Wales in like fourme as it is in this Realm'. This was to be achieved by absorbing the troublesome Marcher Lordships into 13 counties. Twelve of these came under the Welsh Court of Great Sessions with its own system of justice. Monmouthshire, on the other hand, the 13th county, came under the High Court of Chancery in England and the Oxford Circuit. Monmouth was to become the Shire town, and as such was to attract the local gentry for service at the Assizes; as officers in the militia, which was evolving from the trained bands; and as organisers of the social season of races, balls and concerts which was to become a feature of the town in the ensuing centuries.

Although many of the lands of the suppressed priory were going to absentee landlords, the presence of the Somersets at Raglan Castle and the Herberts at Troy House was a magnet to draw lesser gentry to the neighbourhood.

The street plan of Monmouth that John Speede included in 1610 on his county map was to remain almost unaltered until the 19th century.

Overmonnow, with its own church and outer defence of the Clawdd Du ditch and rampart, seems to have developed into something of a faubourg or false borough by the mid-13th century when the ditch was bridged.

The Priory & Two More Churches

By 1101 the priory church, which was built by Benedictine monks from the abbey of Saumur in France, had been dedicated by Bernard, Henry I's chaplain. At the same time a market had been established and burgesses were being attracted by grants of land. By mid-century the triumvirate of lordship, priory and market, from which evolved manor, parish and borough, was beginning to control the town. These three estates are represented on the 15th-century oriel of Monmouth priory by a knight (below left) for the lordship and the protection of the community, by an angel (below centre) for its spiritual welfare, and by a miller (below right) for trade and the creature comforts of the inhabitants.

Towards the end of the 12th century two more churches had been built. Both were dedicated to St. Thomas Becket and appear in documents of 1186. The one at Overmonnow (above right, north door) became a chapel-of-ease to the parish church and was thoroughly restored in the 19th century; the one at Wyesham (above left) evolved into King's Chapel by 1500, Dixton Vicarage by 1740, Wyesham poorhouse in 1815, and a private house in 1890.

Communications

The position of Monmouth, surrounded on three sides by rivers, greatly improved its defensive capability, but meant that for many years its chief link with the outside world was by the river Wye. This was recognised as early as the 13th century by the adoption of a ship for the town's seal (far left). When a new seal was granted in 1675 a ship continued as a centrepiece (left).

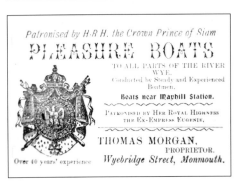

Top: Boats at Llandogo with masts that were hinged at the base to allow them to be lowered to go under bridges.

Middle: Wharves above the Wye bridge c.1840

Heavy goods such as church bells continued to be dragged in barges by bow-hauliers, men harnessed by rope to the barge, and by sail, until the 19th century while stage wagons brought lighter materials from Gloucester and the west. Trade on the river gradually gave way to pleasure trips and nowadays canoeing and rowing by school crews.

Communications

Stagecoaches began to run regularly in the last quarter of the 18th century and reached a peak in 1820. They continued to act as feeders to the railway when it reached Gloucester and only became less important when the Wye Valley Railway from Ross through Monmouth to Chepstow was completed in 1876. This was one of the most beautiful lines in the country. Towards the end of the 19th century Monmouth had two stations, May Hill and Troy. The trains were regular with some six journeys each way between Ross and Monmouth on weekdays and two on Sundays. The line was closed to passenger services on 5 January 1959.

Top: Monmouth May Hill Station, 1958
Above: The derelict Monmouth Troy Station
Right: Details of the last passenger train

The Ministry of Transport replaced the railway with the A40 and in doing so severed Monmouth from its river for the first time in its history. The brutal way in which this was done should be compared with the way local builders created Priory Street as a by-pass in 1837 (see pp. *xii* & 35) and in so doing opened the splendid prospect over the Monnow towards Wales.

MONMOUTH
and its
RAILWAYS

𝕻𝕳𝕺𝕿𝕺𝕲𝖗𝖆𝖕𝖍𝖎𝖈 𝕾𝖔𝖚𝖛𝖊𝖓𝖎𝖗
and
𝕳𝖎𝖘𝖙𝖔𝖗𝖎𝖈𝖆𝖑 𝕹𝖔𝖙𝖊𝖘

in connection with the

LAST PASSENGER TRAIN
on the

**MONMOUTH - ROSS and
MONMOUTH - CHEPSTOW**

branches of the Western Region
of British Railways
(formerly Great Western Railway)

SUNDAY, 4th JANUARY, 1959

Organised by
THE STEPHENSON LOCOMOTIVE SOCIETY
(Midland Area)
being the first Rail-Tour of the Golden Jubilee Year of the Society

The sincerest thanks of the Society are made to Mr. M. D. Greville (*Railway World*, July, 1958), and Rev. W. J. P. Shirehampton, M.A., (*Memorials of Monmouth* No. 6—Railways of Monmouth) for permission to quote historical matter from their articles.

Destroyed by the A40

*Top left and right: The wharf cottages.
They were used by boatmen and there
was an inlet to allow boats to lie near
the cottages*

*Left: Wyebridge Street before its complete
demolition (see also p.39)*

*Left: Chapel Farm, one of the oldest
buildings to be destroyed by the A40.
It was originally a leper hospital,
but by 1427 it had become the
Hospice of St. Michael.
It lay on the Wye opposite Hadnock ford
and the old coach road to Ross went
past it. Its font is in Dixton Church;
all the rest lies under many
tons of concrete*

*Left: The Vega, once one of Monmouth's
most beautifully situated houses on
the Wye and now lost to the A40.
It may have been associated with the
chapel which lay alongside and
at times it housed the boatman
who took passengers across
the river to Hadnock*

Early Cars and Flights

Long before that last train left Monmouth the car had taken over. This was due to the Rolls family, especially Charles Rolls. His father, Lord Llangattock, had asked the Automobile Club to visit The Hendre in 1900 (above left), but by then Charles had moved to higher things and was flying balloons from the town gasworks (above right). Lord Llangattock then offered the Llangattock Plate to the first member of the Aero Club to fly by balloon, airship or plane and land nearest to The Hendre.

TRAGEDY OF THE AIR.

———◆———

HON. C. S. ROLLS KILLED IN AN AEROPLANE DISASTER.

100-FOOT FALL.

———

CRUSHED TO DEATH BEFORE AGONISED ONLOOKERS.

Charles Rolls was killed at Bournemouth in 1910 when his plane dived into the ground when he was landing (left). On his statue outside the Shire Hall (above), he is examining the tail of his plane which was the cause of his death.

While Charles Rolls was ballooning, a local man called Parkes had been building a plane with a 20 hp engine and a wing span of 28 feet. He had previously tried out both a flying bicycle and a flying tricycle unsuccessfully, but with his plane he managed jumps from 10 to 40 feet. But, as he said, it made him feel more like a grasshopper than an aviator!

Timber-framing

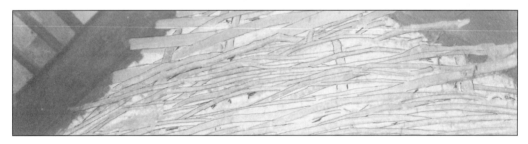

Top left: 7 Church Street

Top right: 19 Church Street

*Middle left: King Henry V,
Monnow Street*

*Centre: Wattle and daub at
22 Drybridge Street*

Bottom: Agincourt House

There are few houses in the town which do not reveal some evidence of timber-framing in their construction and make-up as these examples show. The proximity of the Forest of Dean provided the essential elements for timber-framing, and as towns and villages there grew, the cleared areas allowed the custom to continue. It still flourishes.

Timber-framing

Top left: The Queen's Head in 1889 — as depicted in a watercolour by Mary Bagnall-Oakeley

Middle left: The Queen's Head after the restoration by H.A. Dancey in 1922

Middle right: The inn sign

Bottom left: The Gables in Monk Street, built c.1926

Bottom right: New timber-framed building at Osbaston, installed c.1995

Influential Buildings

Treowen (left), outside Monmouth at Dingestow, probably had a considerable effect on fashion in the town. Of mid-16th century date its importance is the way in which, not only the rooms, but also many of the original features have been preserved — the magnificent staircase, the window cills, the decorated ceilings, the wooden spiral back stair, the panelling, the splendid porch, the huge fireplace and the authentic priest's hole.

Hilston Park (left) belonged to the Needhams in the 17th century, but was destroyed by fire in 1936 and then rebuilt. The long verandahs which were added, set a trend among houses then being built. The ceilings were also decorated.

Courtfield, near Goodrich, was the home of the Vaughan family. Colonel Vaughan commanded the local regiment, The Royal Monmouthshire Royal Engineers with its headquarters at Monmouth Castle. His house set the trend for continuous rail staircases. Its earlier fame was that it housed the reputed cradle of the future Henry V, subsequently moved to Troy House (see p.66).

Influential Buildings — Troy House

There was one way in which the gentry drawn to a county town could be important, and that was by the introduction of new trends in architecture and craftsmanship from the wider world. The 3rd Marquess of Worcester, later to become the 1st Duke of Beaufort, transformed the manor house at Troy into a large mansion in the 1670s while he was building at Badminton and at the castle in Monmouth. Troy is not a very impressive house externally, but it contains good plaster decoration on its ceilings. At one time it contained panelling from Raglan Castle, but this has now been removed to Badminton.

Above: Troy House, north front, c.1670

Left: Entrance to the walled garden

Right: The gateway from the inside of the garden

Influential Buildings — Troy House

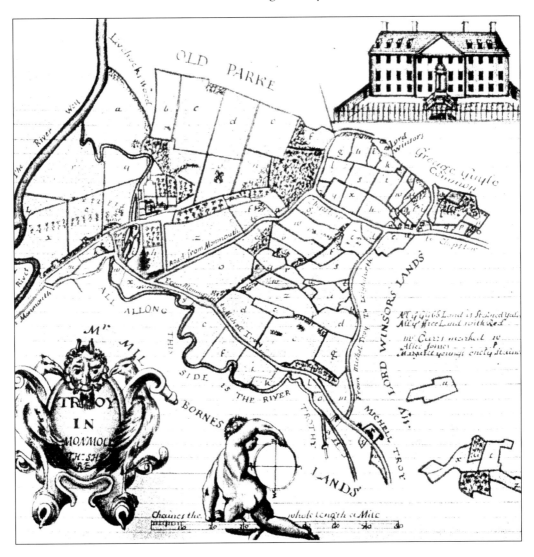

Part of a map of the Troy House Estate in 1712, from a survey of the Manor at Badminton.
It is inscribed:

'In Mitchell Troy and some distance around the Towne of Monmouth theyr customary measure
for land is COVERS, of which 3 make 2 statute acres ... but ye sd woodland is the same as in
England viz. 18ft. to ye Pole or Perch'.

(Cover comes from the Welsh ploughing measure, *Cwfar* and there are several cases
around Dixton of fields called Six Covers, Twelve Covers etc.)

Influential Buildings — Great Castle House

The architectural influence of Troy House was slight, whereas the Somersets' political influence on a small pocket borough was considerable. But Great Castle House, which they built for the comfort of living in the town rather than in the damp surroundings of Troy, was influential both politically and architecturally. The proportions of its Renaissance façade, the flamboyant plaster ceilings, the early dog-leg staircase, the painted overmantel, the window fastenings, often the work of craftsmen employed at Badminton and Troy, set an example for local masons, plasterers and carpenters to emulate.

Great Castle House stands on the site of the round tower demolished after the Civil War and built 'from the great square stones of the gatehouse'. The Earl of Worcester had bought the Lordship of Monmouth for £400 in 1631 and this included the castle with the exception of the Great Hall, which was reserved for the assizes. The house was completed in 1673, but when building at Troy and Badminton had finished the 1st Duke of Beaufort abandoned it as a residence and it was refashioned and repanelled to provide a more comfortable Assize Court that the draughty and damp Great Hall of the castle.

It was a matter of dignity for the Civil and Criminal cases to be held in the same room, the judges sitting at opposite ends to assert the equal importance of both matters. So the first floor of Great Castle House, which consisted of three main rooms and two ante-rooms, had to be converted into a single court-room. Its use as such was short lived, and when the Shire Hall was ready in 1725 the Assizes moved there and the house was let to a maker of drainage pipes and used as the Judges' lodgings. In c.1760 it became a high-class girls' boarding school, but in 1853 the contents of the school were sold and Quarter Sessions rented it for £25 per year and spent £2,000 on converting new wings into a militia store and a residence for the sergeant-major and quartermaster. By 1887 the plaster decoration had been restored and in 1906 the house was acquired by the War Office and has remained the head-quarters of the Royal Monmouthshire Royal Engineers, the senior reserve regiment in the army.

Influential Buildings — Newton Court & Great Osbaston

Above & left: Newton Court, was built by P.M. Hardwick c.1790 and was enlarged for the Dixton squire in c.1800. It was probably designed by Anthony Keck. Using similar brickwork, he also built the Royal Infirmary at Gloucester

Below: Great Osbaston, mainly late 18th century with unique (for Monmouth) chimneys

Influential Buildings — Wyastone Leys

With marvellous views, lying just below the Doward, Wyastone Leys looks down on the Wye. It was rebuilt for J.M. Bannerman by William Burn in 1861. In the 20th century it was divided into flats, but has now been restored by Nimbus Records who not only produce concerts and C.D.s, but have re-hung the tapestries from the earlier house.

Influential Buildings — Wyastone Leys

Above: Tapestry detail

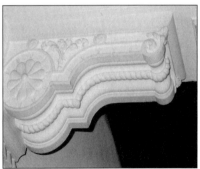

Left & above: The house contains some excellent plasterwork

Influential Houses — Pentwyn

Pentwyn was restored by G.V. Maddox, one of his most elaborate designs. The Maddox family of craftsmen lived in Monmouth and were responsible for many of the better buildings, notably George Vaughan Maddox whose work stands out for assuredness and detailed design.

Influential Houses — The Priory

Fifty years before the Dissolution a fine oriel window was built over an entrance which can still be seen in the masonry (above left & centre rignt). When the Priory was closed in 1536 it was used by a catholic family. In 1768 it was used as a private school and from 1814 housed Monmouth Primary School. The girls used the upper floor and the boys the lower. Sanitation was provided by the river and it was not until 1901 that an inspector 'become sensible to the necessity of erecting a Necessary for the children'. It was not much better when it closed in 1973.

Top left: A drawing by Thomas Tudor in 1815 which shows the building before extensive alterations and additions were made in 1896

Top right: The Priory seal

Middle right: The oriel and blocked doorway

Bottom left: The back of the Priory from the tower of the parish church

Bottom right: The interior after the restoration of 2002

Influential Houses — 1 Agincourt Square

Contemporary with the screen at Treowen (p.19) is 1 Agincourt Square, dated in the apex of the western gable to 1626. Its initials are those of William Roberts whose grandson built Drybridge House in 1671. The carved barge-boards have patterns of dragons to the west and a vine scroll to the north, similar to the carving on the screen at Llandinabo church. Are they, perhaps, part of a screen removed from a local church and eventually used by the thrifty Mr. Roberts to decorate his house in 1626? They have recently been removed and are to be replaced by facsimilies. The following illustrations show the changes that can occur to a façade during an almost 200 year period. The illustration (top left) is by Thomas Tudor, a local artist who toured Wales with Turner and on his return painted many houses in Monmouth, either in watercolours or in brown wash.

Left:
1803

Right:
1865

Left:
1937

Right:
Restored
1991

The Streets

Left: Whitecross Street   Above: Drybridge Street

With the exception of Priory Street (1837) all the main streets in the town had evolved and were named by the middle of the 15th century. As a result almost all houses have been rebuilt several times, usually using the foundations of the older building. But so long as the fashion and taste of the time was accepted, even variations in roof line left the streets harmonious in character, although there might be great variety in the size of the houses.

Whitecross Street and Drybridge Street are good examples of the way in which this uniformity was obtained.

Almost all buildings were originally based on narrow burgage plots, and because street frontage was valuable, the gable ends of buildings erected on these plots faced the street. Many small shops still conform to a single burgage plot, but the larger houses could only be built by incorporating two or three plots, something that became possible when it was safe to live outside the walls.

A good example of a house occupying three burgages is St. James House in Whitecross Street (middle). At the back two of the burgages have survived (left in 1956; right in 2000 with a later extension). The front has an elegant 18th-century brick façade with a hipped roof. A new staircase was inserted *c*.1800 and, to light the landing, a round-headed window was placed over the front door.

The Streets

Top left: Church Street
Top right & middle left: Agincourt Street
Middle right: Almshouse Street

Rounded corners (right — Chippenhamgate St.), were
used to prevent damage by timber wagons (below)
when negotiating the narrow streets.

The Streets

Top left: Granville Street   Top right: Monnow Street in 1970   Middle and bottom left: Monk Street (also known as The Parade) Bottom right: The old road from Monk Street to the Wye. It had been blocked by a gate in 1835, but the original road ran down to the wharves on the river bank

St. James Street

St. James Street contains the Georgian houses of a group of wealthy merchants and burgesses. They have good staircases and interior details. Like many Monmouthshire houses the street front bears little relationship with the back which, in this case, faces the Wye.

Top left: The Grange 1998
Top right: The Grange c.1920
Centre: Two views from the War Memorial
Bottom left: Later development on back of house
*   depicted immediately above*
Bottom right: North side of street

The Shire Hall

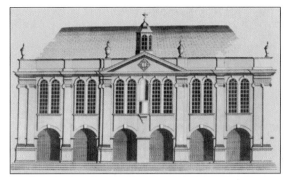

In 1723 the county magistrates decided to build a combined assize court and market hall (left). The architect of this admirable building, that cost £1,700, may well have been Philip Fisher of Bristol, who lived and died in Monmouth.

The design eventually included a rather deplorable statue of Henry V (above) designed by Charles Peart in 1792.

By 1821 the cost of maintenance had become too much for the Corporation and the building was vested in the County. An Act for the Improvement of the Town Hall led, in 1829, to many changes (above right). The work included a grandiose new staircase (below left), rearranged courts (below right), a new cupola and plasterwork, and an extension along Agincourt Street. This cost £6,876, 7s. 4d. plus £143 for furniture and £467 for the Act of Parliament. It resulted in even greater expense through the need to remove the market to a new building in Priory Street. The now abandoned Council Chamber is shown below right.

The Market

Monnow Street (left) is a typical market street, wide in the middle for those selling and narrow at each end to help prevent the animals escaping.

W. H. LANE
(OLD DRURY).

FISHERMEN and
SMOKERS'
RENDEZVOUS

THE SQUARE
MONMOUTH

Before 1601 local farmers sold their corn in Monnow Street (top left). In wet weather this could be unpleasant and the Council decided to provide shelter under the Town Hall and in return to exact a toll on corn measured in their new bushel measure (above left) inscribed 'ELIZABETH DEI GRACIA ANGLIAE FRANCIAE ET HIBERNIAE REGINA'. This charge infuriated the farmers who were welcomed back to the street by W.H. Lane, generally known as Old Drury (above right).

Left: The Market Hall during the fire in 1963. Only the ground floor was saved and now houses the Nelson Museum

The Nelson Museum now holds many of the Town archives and also puts on displays of other subjects than Nelson. Part of the ground floor includes the Citizens' Advice Bureau, where questions on local or personal problems can be answered.

Priory Street & the Slaughterhouses

Monmouth owes a grest deal to the Maddox family, builders and architects, flourishing from *c.*1750 to 1850. The most important was George Vaughan Maddox, who was responsible for the Market Hall, the Methodist Church, Kingsley House, Oak House, the Masonic Lodge, 18 St. James Street, and Priory Street and the slaughterhouses (this page). He also put new galleries in the parish church in 1824.

Above and left: The east side of Priory Street

The slaughterhouses (above & right), which provided the viaduct for Priory Street (top), were built by G.V. Maddox in 1834. It was the classical influence of much of his work that left the town a legacy of good façades and dignified interiors. Unfortunately it was into these slaughterhouses that the lavatories of the school in the Priory emptied down drain pipes.

The Streets

*Right: The Parade
(Monk Street)*

A pair of similar 17th-century houses, occupying several burgage plots, are nos. 6 and 9 in Agincourt Street (below left & right). In both cases the outline of the gable of the central burgage has been incorporated in the façade.

The classical revival came to a blinding halt at Duffryn House in St. Mary Street (left & below), a building that delighted John Betjeman. It has been at times a fit-up theatre for travelling players and a Nonconformist Meeting House. There are traces of its former uses; the theatre being more elaborate than the Nonconformist Meeting House. It is now a private house.

Plan of Monmouth from a Survey by John Wood, 1835

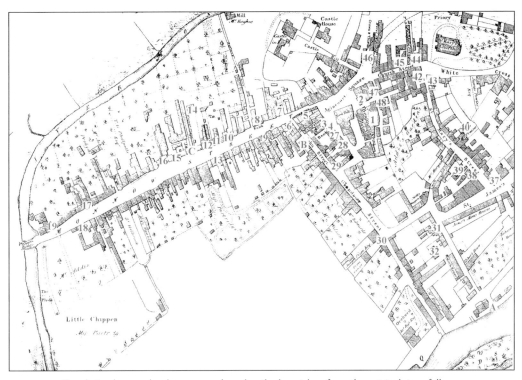

For clarity the map has been renumbered — the key, taken from the original, is as follows:

REFERENCES

Nº		Nº	
1	Beaufort Arms Hotel and Posting House	35	White Hart
2	The Bull	36	Queen's Head
3	King's Head	37	Gloucestershire House
4	Bank — Messrs. Jones, Davies & Co	38	Carpenter's Arms
5	Post Office	39	Independent Chapel
b	Black Swan	40	Roman Catholic Do
6	Talion	41	Crown & Sceptre
7	Fountain	42	Angel Inn
8	Bank — Bromage, Snead & Co	43	Griffin
9	Nag's Head	44	Bell
10	White Lion	45	White Swan
11	Boar's Head	46	Crown & Thistle
12	King's Arms	e	Reformers' Tavern
13	Butcher's Arms	47	Cross Keys
14	Baptist Chapel	48	Golden Ball
c	Vine Tree	A	Site of St Johns Monastery
15	Merlin Printing Office	B	Site of the Hospital of the Holy Trinity
f	Rope Makers' Arms	C	Burial Ground of th..

37

Brackets

Top left: The Gables, Monk Street

*Top centre: The Grange,
St. James Street*

*Top right: The Gatehouse,
Monk Street*

Left: North Parade House

*Right: Priory House
(Conservative Club)*

Bottom left: Whitecross Street

Bottom right: Church Street

Slum Clearance

Between 1801 and 1831, the population grew by about 1,500. Many of these people were housed in courts, built in the gardens of burgesses, with an entry through a passage from the street. In the 1950s many of these courts were demolished in the name of slum clearance. The doctrine, that it was cheaper to destroy and rebuild than to repair, led to the complete destruction of Wyebridge Street (below) which included a pair of delightful 18th-century houses (right). They have been replaced by a patch of municipal grass.

Slum clearance became important because the influx of the motor car made street widening necessary. In some cases it meant the narrowing of the pavements (church side of Priory Street). It led to the current problem that the pedestrian has had to give way to the motorist or be killed.

Drybridge Terrace

Drybridge Terrace was originally known as Tyler's Terrace and was one of the courts of terraces built at the back of the main streets to house the increasing population during the 19th century.

Almost all of these courts were demolished between the two world wars and afterwards. Drybridge Terrace, leading back from Drybridge Street, was saved by a far-sighted benefactor and is now one of the most delightful terraces in the town. It seems to have been built in two parts which are linked by a splendid Neo-Gothic cottage (above right and bottom left).

Terraces

The movement from the town centre and living over the shop began for the wealthier burgesses in the second half of the 19th century. Monkswell Road (above right, left and below) was built in three parts between 1869 and the end of the century, Rock Crescent and North Parade Terrace at each end with Claremont filling the gap. The house (top right) is lower down Monkswell Road. A movement with more serious consequences was the development of the suburbs at Osbaston, Wyesham and Overmonnow.

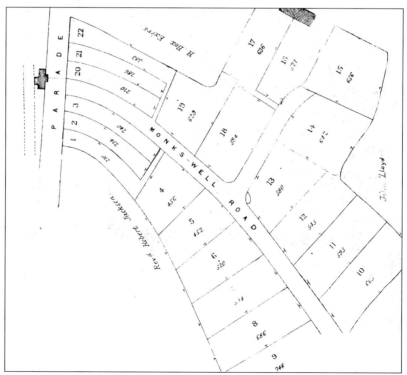

Turnpike Houses

Although the Monmouth Turnpike Trust was set up in 1755, most of the Pike houses date from the 19th century.

Top: Wyesham c.1836, since demolished

Middle: Hereford Road c.1840

Bottom: Drybridge. It involved the conversion of an existing 17th-century building c.1840

Turnpike Houses

Top: Dixton c.1800. The side and back lightened with Neo-Gothic windows in c.1900. It was even more necessary when the embankment of the A40 cut out the view to the south. It is now a private house

Above: Lydart, one of the larger pike houses, having to deal with heavy traffic from three directions

Left: Dixton Gate (The Burgage) 19th century. Like Dixton adapted from an earlier building

The Inns of Monmouth

In the Middle Ages Monmouth had its own vineyard, while at the time of the Domesday survey rent was being paid in honey, the chief ingredient of mead. Most ale was brewed at home, but if it was brewed for sale the castle exacted a toll of 17 gallons for every brew. By the 16th century a rough licensing system had been introduced, and by 1722, when it was estimated that the average consumption of ale for every man, woman and child was about 36 gallons a year, there were 85 alehouses in Monmouth:

Wyesham — 5; Overmonnow — 11; Wyebridge Ward — 23; Monnow Street — 22
The Square and Church Street — 24

By 1850 the number was only slightly less — 72 — and a writer to the local paper complained that 'about £50,000 was being spent annually in these establishments, money which would be far better spent in getting a railway in the town'. In fact, when Troy Station was built, a bar was the first part to be opened!

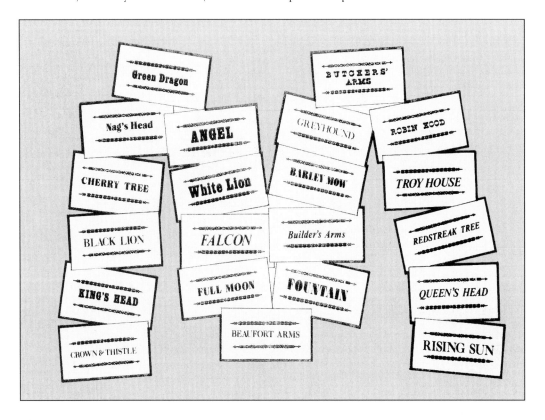

Some idea of the number of inns that Monmouth used to have can be seen by the list of beer tickets (above) that Benjamin Hall issued when electioneering for Parliament in 1831. In the same election Hall's opponent, the Marquis of Worcester, spent £892 16s. 1d. on innkeepers' bills alone.

The Inns of Monmouth

The Griffin, with its rounded corner (top left), is opposite the Angel (top right), which has the longest known documentary history of a Monmouth inn. It was a workshop at the end of the 13th century, had become a parish church brewhouse by the 16th, and an inn by 1700. It is now a shop again. The Old Nag's Head (bottom) is built into one of the bastions of the medieval Dixton Gate.

The Inns of Monmouth

Right: The Black Lion, No. 19 St. Mary Street, in 1995

Top: It had a much better façade as designed by the architect in 1860

Left: 16 Drybridge Street, which now provides bed and breakfast, was once the Red Lion Inn

The Inns of Monmouth

Top: The Queen's Head

Whitecross House (bottom left), once the Portcullis Inn, is very similar to 16 Drybridge Street (p.46 opposite). Both date from the late 17th century and were once important inns.

It is said that narrow passages, such as Inch Lane (bottom right), were designed to provide a safe way for those who had drunk too much to get from one street to another, as they were narrow enough to feel the walls on both sides. There were three 'Inch Lanes' in Monmouth.

The Inns of Monmouth

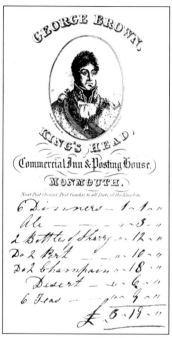

The King's Head (above c.1900), became important as a posting inn during the lattter part of the 17th century. The landlord at that time was Richard Ballard, a Royalist, who was postmaster and also mayor in 1675. As landlord he issued silver tokens with the words 'God Preserve Our Gracious King' and the bust of Charles II.

The account (above), shows that dinner and tea for six people in 1830, with ample sherry, port and champagne, cost £6 18s.

During the late 18th and early 19th centuries coaches left the King's Head (below) for London, and later (left) to meet the Parliamentary Cheap Train at Gloucester on its way to London.

The overmantel in the bar seems to be an amalgam of Charles I and Charles II, and is an almost exact vernacular contemporary (1673-1675) of the professional but pedestrian one in Castle House (see p.120).

Monmouth, Ross, and Gloucester.

THE Public are respectfully informed that on and after MONDAY, the 11th inst.,

The "Mazeppa" Fast Coach,

Will leave the BEAUFORT ARMS and KING'S HEAD HOTELS, MONMOUTH, every Morning, Sundays excepted, at a Quarter before Seven ; passing through Ross and arriving in Gloucester at Ten, in time for the Parliamentary Cheap Train that leaves the Station at 27 minutes past 10.

Fares throughout to London 14s. 7d.

On its return it will leave the Station at Half-past Four, and Heath's Office, and Bell Hotel, Five minutes afterwards, immediately after the arrival of Trains from London, Manchester, Liverpool, and Bristol.

This Coach affords an accommodation long desired as it is the only conveyance that leaves Monmouth in time for the Parliamentary Train, by which Passengers can reach any station for 1d. per mile.

June 5th.   BARRETT & CO., Proprietors

New Coach
TO
LONDON,
THE
PAUL PRY
Through Ross, Gloucester, Cheltenham, and Oxford, from the
King's Head Hotel, Monmouth,
Every Day at One, (Sundays excepted.)—Leaves the Blossoms' Inn, Lawrence Lane, London, at Six in the Evening, and arrives in Monmouth by Twelve the following Day.
ROBERTSON & Co. Proprietors

The King's Head

The King's Head now includes the Monmouth Bank (above right) and the County Club (above left), with its oriel window. The latter was built by T.H. Wyatt in 1877. The inn was built on the outer bailey ditch of the castle; as a result the back of the building (right) has one storey below the level of the ground floor at the front.

When the inn was for sale in 1840 it contained 18 bedrooms, 4 sitting rooms and an assembly room. There was also a copper furnace and 'a four-motion beer and cider engine'. The stables included 16 coach horses, several carriages, a hearse, and a superior mourning coach.

The inn caught fire in 1870, but survived, and was sold for £1,600 in 1909.

Getting to London became much easier when the station at Gloucester had opened and coaches from Monmouth could meet trains and send or bring back passengers from far and wide.

The Beaufort Arms

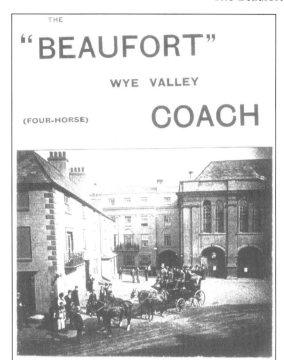

THE PUBLIC ARE RESPECTFULLY INFORMED

THE "MAZEPPA," COACH

WILL leave the BEAUFORT ARMS, MONMOUTH, (Sundays excepted), every Morning at a Quarter past Six o'clock, (London time) to meet the following Trains :—

BIRMINGHAM . . 9 38
LONDON 10 17
BRISTOL 10 29

and return the same Evening at Five o'clock from the Gloucester Station and Heath's Office.

FARES :—

INSIDE, 5s.   OUTSIDE, 3s.

HEATH & CO., Proprietors.

According to Heath (1799), this inn consisted originally of two small tenements, one a butcher's and the other a corn dealer's. What is now the yard was a fives court.

The Beaufort Arms became important after the building of the Shire Hall in 1724. Through the influence of the Duke it acquired a part of that new building which encroached on the inn's fives court. It became the chief coaching inn, and when Mr. Tibbs acquired it in the late 18th century he added to its attractions by building a bridge over the Monnow and laying out pleasure gardens, a bowling green and river walks along Vauxhall which were so enjoyed by Torrington and John Wesley.

The inn reached its peak during the early 19th century when the Wye Tour was popular and when Nelson had given it publicity by staying there.

When offered for sale in 1839 it included '36 bedrooms, 9 sitting rooms, 38 four-poster beds, 50 horses, and 18 carriages with their harness'. The sale also included full length portraits of George III and Queen Charlotte by Drummond.

The hotel has lately been converted into Beaufort Court with shops and apartments.

The Beaufort Arms

BILL OF FARE FOR THE MAYOR OF MONMOUTH'S DINNER, (Mr. Silas Blandford, October 4th, 1773.)	£.	s.	d.
15 Couple Ducks	1	8	0
2 Necks Pork	0	15	0
8 Rumps and 3 Ribs Beef	4	12	9
8 Hams	3	16	0
23 Couples Fowls, 1s. 4d.	1	10	8
8 Turkies	1	1	0
16 Pigeons	0	6	0
2 Loins Veal	1	0	0
Mutton for Pasties	0	2	6
Veal for Stuffing ye Turkies	0	2	6
Flour for Puddings and Pastry	0	12	0
5 Puddings for ye dinner and 3 to have cold	1	2	0
Brandy for the Puddings	0	0	6
8lb. Suet for the Puddings	0	2	8
40lb. Butter, at 8d.	1	6	8
4 dishes Scotch Collops	0	7	0
Grocery	0	19	9
Baking the Pastries	0	5	0
Dressing the Dinner	3	3	0
3 Women's Hire	0	4	0
Gave the Cook	0	5	0
Servants	0	5	0
18lb. Bacon	0	12	0
Bread	1	7	0
Mustard	0	0	6
112 gallons Ale, at 1s. per gallon	5	12	0
12 Tongues	0	18	0
9 Apple Pies	0	18	0
6 Damson Pies	0	12	0
10 doz. Cheese Cakes and Tarts	0	15	0
6 Geese	0	18	0
	£34	19	6

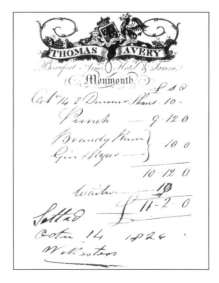

Top left: Mr. J. Chilcott was the toast master at the inn in Regency times

Top right: The bill of fare for the Mayor of Monmouth's Dinner in 1773. In case this was not enough the Duke of Beaufort gave two fat bucks, Mr. Hughes of Treaddam three brace of carp and one of tench, Sir John Stepney several flat fish, Mr. Kemeys 14 bottles of Jamaica Rum, and there was wine, spirits and game from 'individuals innumerable'

Middle left: A meal about 1792. The billhead includes the Duke's arms

Right: A bill for dinner for two in 1826

The Inns of Monmouth

The Punch House (above) and the Bull are in Agincourt Square. The former was known as the Wine Vaults in 1769 (below left). The profusion of pubs in the Square gave rise to the rhyme: 'A gin court here, a gin court there, no wonder they call it Agincourt Square'!

Middle right: Only the sign board remains of what was the Full Moon near Monnow Bridge (bottom right)

The Inns of Monmouth

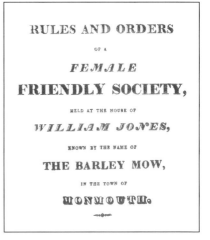

RULES AND ORDERS

OF A

FEMALE

FRIENDLY SOCIETY,

HELD AT THE HOUSE OF

WILLIAM JONES,

KNOWN BY THE NAME OF

THE BARLEY MOW,

IN THE TOWN OF

MONMOUTH.

The Barley Mow (top left) was one of Monmouth's best known inns. It has remained in the same building for almost 200 years. One of the most important functions of the inns was to house a Friendly Society. During the 19th century there were at least 33 in Monmouth, both male and female. Each had their own rules and were an early form of insurance against sickness and death. There was a flourishing female society at the Barley Mow (top right).

The amount of drink consumed was often considerable. The vicar of Overmonnow entered the fray in 1883 when he said it was disgraceful that at the Mayor's luncheon, 21 men 'the so called elite of the town, had managed to drink 48 bottles of champagne as well as other wines'. A similar number of bottles, usually quart ones, graced the Mayor's table on other occasions throughout the century.

The Robin Hood (below), which was built *c.*1580, is structurally the oldest inn in the town. An early inn sign read:

'Walk in, kind sirs, my Ale is Good.
And take a pot with Robin Hood
If Robin Hood is not at Home
Pray take a pot with Little John'.

Hyam's Mineral Waters

JOHN B. HYAM,

Mineral Water Manufacturer,

GLENDOWER STREET.
MONMOUTH

13

"For upwards of six months I have used
no Seltzer Water but Mr. Hyam's, of Monmouth. A great quantity has been consumed
in this house, and I have found it most excellent. I never have been so well supplied.

BEAUFORT.

Hyam's Mineral Water shop was In Monnow Street (top left). It was designed by Lawrence of Newport and built by Lewis of Monmouth in 1866. The new building, of Freestone with Aberdeen granite pillars, was widely praised at the time. The spandrels (centre) were elaborately carved and it was one of the first shops in Monmouth to introduce curved plate glass windows. The shop later became W.H. Smith's and is now 'Salt and Pepper'. Mr. Hyam also owned the Mineral Water Works in Glendower Street (top right).

Advertising was obviously of first class importance as Mr. Hyam's card (above right) and the specially printed card from the Duke of Beaufort (lower right) both testify. Envelopes, then as now, were also a good source of advertisement as the envelope posted in Monmouth in 1892 demonstrates (above left).

Houses

 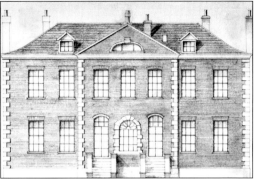

Cornwall House was built in several stages and occupies the sites of at least three burgages. In 1678, when it was called the Great House, it belonged to George Milborne. By 1699 it had come into the possession of Thomas Brewer, a blacksmith. It was acquired in 1752 by Henry Burgh, the Duke of Beaufort's agent, and he added the fine front facing Chippenham (above right) that year. At the bottom of the garden, which included the town butts, the agent built a grandstand for the Duke and his friends to watch the races which took place on Chippenham. In the 1770s the street front took its present form, the porch, side doors and fanlights being added *c.*1800 (above left).

Overmonnow House, St. Thomas Square (above), was once the vicarage and has a round-headed window with Gothic glazing bars similar to those on the Royal George. This window does not light the splendid staircase which is at the back of the large central hall. It is an example of the quality of many 19th-century vicarages, accommodating a large family and many servants.

The Gatehouse in Monk Street (above left) stands on the site of Monks Gate and has a pleasantly recessed Greek Revival porch. Over it is a protruding oriel, inserted between the wars so that the ladies who lived there would have better views of what was going on in the street.

Lloyds Bank & Chippenham House

The building that now houses Lloyds Bank (left) was built in the 18th century with a walled garden at the back. Philip Fisher, the possible architect of the Shire Hall lived here, as did his relative, P.M. Hardwick, who organised the building of the Round House and the Naval Temple on the Kymin.

The summer house (above) lay in the garden of the house adjoining. It was here that Nelson is said to have had coffee before going up the Kymin to view the Naval Temple. This is how it looked in 1860, but it has since suffered some alterations.

Chippenham House (above & right — the garden front) is of late 18th-century date and was the home of many doctors, including Dr. Holbrook, from early in the 19th century.

Chapel House, The Parade

Chapel House is a large, externally plain building with little to break the regularity of its features apart from some prominent plumbing! It dates from the late 17th and early 18th centuries and overlooks the Monnow. It has decorated plaster ceilings (below right), a fine open-well staircase with twisted balusters (below left), a well-panelled room and a fireback of 1720 with the initials of William Rea, an ironmaster and former Mayor of Monmouth (see p.121). According to Charles Heath the house obtained its Georgian features from another ironmaster, David Tanner, 'who gave the house its present handsome appearance'.

Top left: The street front

Left: The garden front, overlooking the river

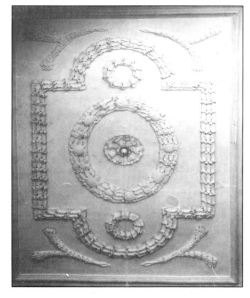

Houses

Above: Singleton House in Monk Street

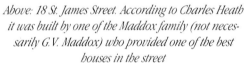

Above: 18 St. James Street. According to Charles Heath it was built by one of the Maddox family (not necessarily G.V. Maddox) who provided one of the best houses in the street

*Above and right: The Grange Coach House.
It is built of brick and includes a long passage leading to the rear of the house. It was very convenient for Wye Bridge and the Chepstow road.
The Grange itself is now part of Monmouth School*

Houses — Monk Street

Top left: Kingsley House & Hendre House c.1830

Centre right: In 1846 G.V.Maddox converted a small Georgian theatre into the Masonic Lodge

Centre left: Oak House, built in 1846, had a good garden at the back. This was ruined when it became the Telephone Exchange with some dreadful buildings replacing the garden

Bottom left and right: Parade House is of 18th-century date and was originally the Harp Inn. It was converted by a local banker in the mid-19th century. He introduced the Gothicised windows and the splendid staircase. It is one of the few houses in the town with a pleasantly hipped roof. It is now a residential home and has a good garden at the back

The Royal George, Monk Street

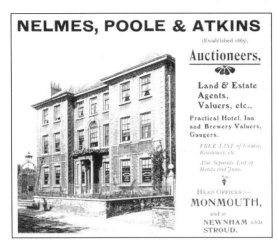

The Royal George in Monk Street is a fine early Georgian house which was given a neo-classical interior by the commander of the Monmouthshire Militia about 1800. It was for sale in 1900 (top left) and recently has suffered a period of neglect (middle left), but restoration has now taken place (top right). It has some fine decorated pillars in the ground floor, good windows and good stairs. It is now an excellent retirement home with a pleasant garden and extensive forecourt.

Drybridge House, Overmonnow

Drybridge House (above) has inscriptions above the door stating that it was built in 1671 and restored in 1867. The earliest building was the work of William Roberts (of Monmouth and Greys Inn), Receiver and Paymaster of the works at Windsor throughout the great period of remodelling by Hugh May and Sir Christopher Wren. His grandfather's initials are said to be in the apex of the gable of 1 Agincourt Square. The restoration and enlargement in 1867 was carried out by C.H. Crompton Roberts who retained what was left of the old house — the fine chimney piece with fruit and leaves carved in the style of Grinling Gibbons, the panelling and the plaster ceiling which has much in common with that at Treowen. The restoration also included a series of windows painted in grisaille showing the story of King Arthur (p.118) The exterior abounds with shields and carvings and there is a pleasant 19th-century brick stable-block. The house had delightful gardens and a first-class cricket ground. The family did much for Overmonnow both financially and socially.

North Parade House

*Above: The cottages, warehouse
and dwelling that comprised
North Parade House*

Left: Inside the warehouse

This is one of the most architecturally satisfactory houses in Monmouth and is largely the work of an enterprising wool merchant who knew what he wanted and saw that he got it. He converted an existing 18th-century house into a comfortable family home with Adam-style fireplaces in several rooms, a continuous rail stairway lit by a cupola and a beautiful walled garden at the back. The adjoining malthouse he converted into a warehouse with benches and racks for storing his wool. To the north he bought four cottages for his workforce and provided a discrete walled access to their place of work. It is a well preserved example of the way in which business, industry and family life can be combined if the will and the taste are there.

BUILDINGS AND STREETS

The County Gaol, Hereford Road

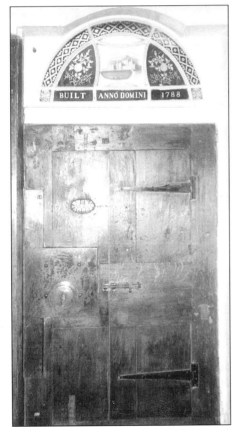

Above: The view on the Hereford Road in 1860, showing the toll house, gaol before demolition, and North Parade House on the right

Left: The back door of the gatehouse of the gaol with a stained glass fanlight

The view from North Parade House was dramatically changed in 1790 when the walls of the new county gaol began to rise. Built by William Blackburn, with advice from John Howard, it was designed as a model prison. However, it was viewed with distaste by the occupants of the elegant houses on The Parade. The contractor for the gaol was John Fentiman and the cost was about £5,000. It was closed in 1869 and only the gatehouse, with the condemned cells over, and a stained glass fanlight showing it as conceived in 1788, remain.

The gaol held 204 inmates and contained chapel, school and baths. It is now part of Monmouth School for Girls.

The Rolls Hall

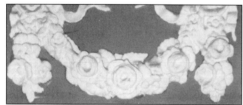

The Rolls Hall was presented to the people of Monmouth by J.A. Rolls to commemorate the golden jubilee of Queen Victoria. The architect was F.A. Powell and the cost was £8,000. In 1992 it was converted from a concert hall to a public library. The original design (centre above) contrasts with the modern lighting system suspended from open metal-work (left).

Unusual buildings

Priory House, Whitecross Street (left and below). This house has suffered many alterations since it became the Monmouth Classical Academy in the first quarter of the 19th century; it is now the Conservative Club.

In 1840 Lord Llangattock provided £1,000 towards a hospital in Monmouth to replace the Dispensary in St. James Street. The ground was bought from the Duke of Beaufort for £250. It was designed by Richard Creed, built by Collins and Geoffrey, and George Edwards of Monmouth furnished it. It is a delightful building, light and pleasant; a place to get better in rather than to die. It was opened in 1902, some 60 years after it had been proposed, but it was well worth waiting for.

Monmouth Union Workhouse (left), was built in the 1870s for 240 inmates at a cost of £10,000. It is now part of Monmouth School for Girls.

Left: A pauper's gravestone, Monmouth cemetery

Once the vicarage and now part of Monmouth School for Girls, St. Katherine's is a curious mixture of stone from the gaol and brick from the neighbouring brickyard. The recesses in a side wall (below) may have been part of the gaol.

Victorian restoration & luxury

Wyastone Leys (above) was rebuilt for J.M. Bannerman by William Burn in 1861. Neither this, nor Dingestow (left) had much influence architecturally, but the Bosanquets, through their interest in music, cricket, the magistracy and such organisations as the Working Men's Institute, played an important part in the social life of Monmouth.

Dingestow Court (above) was restored and rebuilt for S. Bosanquet by Lewis Vulliamy in 1845, with additions by J.P. Seddon in 1859.

Middle left: The Oak room at Troy House with the cradle in which Henry V, when a baby, is supposed to have slept
Middle right: The main hall at Dingestow Court
Left: The servants at The Hendre c.1890

Becoming a servant at The Hendre, the largest Victorian house in the district, was something to be proud of. They were well treated, well fed and had good bedrooms. But they had to get up early, go to bed early and, above all, behave!

Schools and Almshouses

Monmouth School (top) and almshouses (middle) were founded by William Jones in 1614 and built and controlled by the Haberdashers Company. The original almshouses and school were built of brick, a medium rarely used in Monmouth. The almshouses were rebuilt by J.B. Bunning in 1842 and added to by William Burn in 1895/6. They were eventually replaced by new almshouses behind the Rolls Hall (left) in 1961.

Schools

Above & right: Monmouth School for Girls founded 1892.
In 1897 the Haberdashers, on a splendid site on the Hereford Road,
employed Henry Stock to build a new school

Left: Glendower Street
Board School, 1875

Built by David Roberts, whose
name is carved below the
central finial, this is now
Monmouth School's
Music Department

Left: The Jones Endowed
Elementary School, 1906.
This was built by Henry
Stock, the architect of
Monmouth School for Girls,
and is now part of
Monmouth Comprehensive
School

St. Mary's parish church

Above: The church in 1684 by Thomas Dineley
Right: The 14th-century west door and window
Below: Fragment of 12th-century string course on tower

A little later than the construction of the Shire Hall came the rebuilding of the parish church, which was still using what was left of the priory. In 1730 it was described as too small, ruinous in roof, walls and foundations, and so decayed that unless it was replaced the parish 'must be destitute of a place for the worship of Almighty God'. So the churchwardens commissioned two masons, two carpenters, two glaziers and two plasterers to report on its condition and estimate the cost of rebuilding. As a result of their report a petition was presented to the king asking for a Brief (an order giving authority) for collections throughout the kingdom towards the cost. By 1731 Francis Smith of Warwick had been appointed as architect, with instructions to retain the tower and spire and as much of the old walling as possible.

Smith's auditory church with its Tuscan columns was something quite new and inevitably caused criticism. This was fuelled by trouble over the cost. The church had been opened in 1737, but by 1743 only £1,552 had been collected and the sum due was £1,994. It was eventually paid, but only after a list of the names of people who had promised and failed to subscribe was placed in the porch. It contained two columns headed 'Sperate' (Hopeful) and 'Desperate' (Hopeless). By 1743 Nathaniel Wilkinson of Worcester had rebuilt the spire, crowning it with the Corinthian capital now inside the church.

St. Mary's parish church

Left: Francis Smith of Warwick's church
Above: The Georgian church with its Tuscan pillars

George Street, at the vicar's request, came to Monmouth in 1879 to give his opinion on Francis Smith's building. He found it 'deplorably bad in every respect ... dark, dismal, badly seated and badly ventilated ... no style at all ... extremely unattractive and uninteresting'. He left an estimate of £22,000 for rebuilding, later reduced to between £5,000 and £6,000, being all the parish could find. A contract was signed with Wall and Hook of Brinscombe and the church was closed in June 1881. Street died before completion and the church was finished by his clerk of works, Richard Creed.

The carving was carried out by H. Frith of Gloucester; H.H. Martyn and William Letheren collaborated on the wood and ironwork of the screen, and C.E. Kempe was asked to provide eight of the windows. The church was reopened in November 1882.

It has been pointed out that had Street's original plan been possible then Monmouth might have had a larger church than Newport. It could then have hosted the cathedral of the diocese and might have remained the County town.

The only window in the church not by Kempe is shown on the left. Designed by Revd. B.F.L. Clarke, a former curate of St. Mary's, it depicts Withenhoc, a founder of the Norman priory; Geoffrey of Monmouth, the celebrated historian; Francis Smith, the architect of the Georgian church, and George Edmund Street, architect of the present building. St Mary's in different guises, appears in each picture. By contrast with the other aisle windows there are clear glass quarries in the lattice lead-work.

St. Mary's parish church

Top left: Masons' carving on the tower parapet
Top right: St. Mary's church in 2000
Centre left: The pulpit by Franklin of Deddington
Bottom: The altar in the Lady Chapel with the riddel posts
with curious brass bases, probably by Letheren and Martin
of Cheltenham, who made the gates

St. Mary's parish church

Top left: Marble tablet to Philip Fisher (d. 1776), possibly the architect of the Shire Hall, and P.M. Hardwick (d.1818), who was largely responsible for building the Round House and Naval Temple on the Kymin

Middle left: Marble memorial to Lord Llangattock (d. 1911), who was Monmouth's greatest benefactor. The portrait bust is the work of Goscombe John who also designed the statue of his son, Charles Rolls, in the Square

Bottom left: A strange memorial with sails, mast, anchor, well-fed child, elephant's trunk etc. to Joseph Price (d.1796). The rather obscure symbolism seems to commemorate his naval service against France and his more

lucrative post of Marine Paymaster and Naval Storekeeper to the East India Company. The Price family kept slaves and the Parish Register records the baptism in 1763 of Andrew Davis and Joseph Monmouth, 'blacks belonging to Mr. Price' and, in 1795, 'Thomas, an East Indian servant of Mr. Price'. The memorial is an early work of Sir Richard Westmacott, but not one of his best

Top right: The finest monument in the church. Elaborate cartouche with cherub and skull, swags, coronet and arms to John and Elizabeth Hoskins (d.1715 and 1699 respectively). The Revd. James Scudamore (d.1713) and Dorothy Hoskins (d.1743) erected the monument. The first two were recusants; James Scudamore was vicar of Dixton. There is no reference to the burial of Elizabeth Hoskins in the register of this church, but the Dixton register records in Scudamore's writing that she was buried 'at about 12 of the clock at night in St. Mary's church'. Many local recusants were buried at night, in this case presumably with the connivance of the vicar.

St. Mary's parish church

Many of the windows in St. Mary's church, including those on this page, are by Charles Eamer Kempe (and Kempe & Co.) and were made between 1882 and 1920. The most important is at the west end over what was the baptistry — known as the 'four rivers window'.

Top left: Lady chapel. Pilate denouncing Christ

Top centre: North aisle. David (Wales); Patrick (Ireland); Alfred (England) and Margaret (Scotland)

Top right: In memory of the officers and other ranks who gave up their lives during the Great War 1914-1918

Bottom left: The 1902 Memorial of the Boer War. It shows Henry V, the Monnow bridge and the Town Seal. It is overlooked in the upper light by St. Denys, of all people, with the arms of France

St. Peter's church, Dixton

Although well inside Monmouth Borough and County boundaries, Dixton church (top) has been in the diocese of Hereford for most of the last 800 years. It was restored three times in the 19th century; in 1824 the box pews and three-decker pulpit were removed and the Laudian communion rails were put in their present position; in 1851 the Norman chancel arch was replaced by a Gothic one; and in 1861 Prichard and Seddon removed the gallery, laid new tiles, removed the Romanesque (?) carving from the font and rebuilt the south porch, the old one becoming the front door of the rectory (above).

St. Peter's church, Dixton

Above left: One of the oil lamps which were used to light the church not very long ago

Above right: The Royal Arms of Queen Anne, 1711. Dixton is the only Monmouth church to have retained its Royal Arms

Left: Design for the organ case by J.P. Seddon

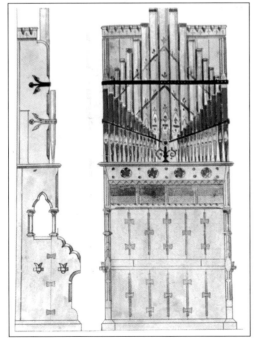

Bottom right: Acrostic gravestone to John Renie (d.1832). His name appears 46,000 times in an attempt to deceive the devil

St. Thomas the Martyr church, Overmonnow

St. Thomas's church by John Arthur Evans c.1900

The chancel arch   *The side door*

St. Thomas the Martyr church, Overmonnow

The print above, of *c.*1850, shows St. Thomas's church after its first restoration. The curious turret was replaced by the present belfry and the stump of the cross, lying by the roadside, was moved into the centre of the square in 1888. The new shaft (left) was designed by the architect F.A. Powell and carved by H. Wall of Newport. It was paid for by C.H. Crompton-Roberts of Drybridge House.

The vestry, on the far left, was also designed by F.A. Powell in 1888.

The restoration of the Anglican churches began at Dixton in 1823 and followed at Overmonnow in 1831. The work at Dixton continued throughout the century and involved the conflicting views of a series of incumbents, whilst in 1829 St. Thomas at Overmonnow had been condemned by the bishop as 'this dilapidated and forsaken church'. Arthur Wyatt, the Duke's agent at Troy, undertook the restoration task in cooperation with his nephew T.H. Wyatt. He was followed by a number of architects including Prichard & Seddon, F. Mew and F.A. Powell, all of whom had trouble with the clergy employing them.

St. John's church, The Buckholt

St. John's church at The Buckholt (top and left) was built by W. Simmons in 1889.

The church's font (right) is said to have been found at Dixton. The rim is inscribed:
1663 DAVID FOX, DAVID WILLIAM, GEORGE PHIELIPE, CHURCH WARDENS

St. Mary's Roman Catholic church, Monmouth

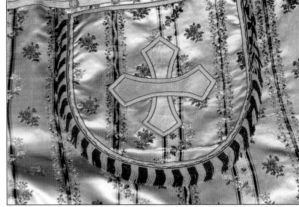

Many influential Catholic families took the oath at Quarter Sessions to comply with the Relief Act of 1778, and in 1793 an influential group commissioned Michael Watkins, the landlord of the Robin Hood Inn, to build a chapel in St. Mary's Street. He had to conform to the Corporation's conditions that it should be hidden from the street and not look like a church. It took nearly 100 years and a series of Relief Acts to acquire a small tower and bells, and for it to become visible from the street. In 1861 it was decided to build 'a new church and school' and this was completed in 1871. It entailed the removal of the cottages hiding the church and the construction of the tower and west end (left). The builders were paid £530 and the architect, Benjamin Bucknall, £39 in instalments. There is a rather sad memorandum from the appropriately named Father Abbot, the priest: 'There has been nothing paid to Thos. Abbot for board and lodging of the architect during his 35 days of residence, inspecting and directing the work: at 2s. 6d. per day would have been £4 7s. 6d.'.

The cope (top right) was made from the dress in which Gladstone's sister was presented at court. The processional cross (centre) is 14th century and the wooden crucifix (right) with linen loin cloth and arms hinged at the shoulders for use when placing the body in an Easter sepulchre is possibly 17th century and of Spanish origin.

St. James church, Wyesham

St. James was completed in 1876 to a design by J.P. Seddon to replace the 12th-century church of St. Thomas Becket, that became progressively a vicarage, parish poor house and private dwelling. The tower was completed in 1891 (left), but has since been truncated (above).

The drawing and plan (opposite) appeared in *The Architect* in 1872.

In 1885 the building was described as 'studiously plain, but well suited to the lovely pastoral site it occupies and forms a pleasing group with the schools alongside, both by the same architect'. The church contains a typical Seddon reredos (below).

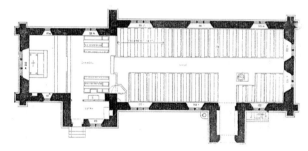

The Methodist Church, St. James Street

In many ways the Methodist church in St. James Street, designed by G.V. Maddox in 1837 (left), displays typical nonconformist conformity, typified with the design of the gallery and organ loft (below) and the gallery seating (above).

The Baptist Chapel, Monk Street

The Baptists began in a small brick building off Monnow Street. It was opened in 1818 and enlarged in 1836. In 1851 there were 80 present in the morning, 130 in the evening and 50 children. 'Far below normal', grumbled the minister.

In 1906 the foundation stone of a new church in Monk Street was laid out and the building was opened in 1907. The architect was B. Lawrence, the contractor G. Jones and the driving force behind the scheme was Mr. Sambrook, all of Monmouth.

At the opening Mr. Sambrook, with a glance across the road at the parish church, remarked that the Baptists were true to God's word and had 'no new theology in them'.

The Independent Congregational Chapel, Glendower Street

The chapel, opened in 1844, was designed by William Armstrong of Bristol and built by B. Lawrence of Monmouth. The side galleries were added in 1855. It was the only chapel in Monmouth to have its own graveyard.

The Independent Congregational Chapel, Glendower Street

The building ceased to be used as a chapel and deteriorated badly (see previous page) until it was splendidly restored by Mr. and Mrs. Anthony Sully in 2002 who, as interior designers, designed the conversion into a private house under the direction of the architect, Graham Frecknall.

Top: The lounge

Left: View of the kitchen/breakfast area from the lounge

The Independent Congregational Chapel, Glendower Street

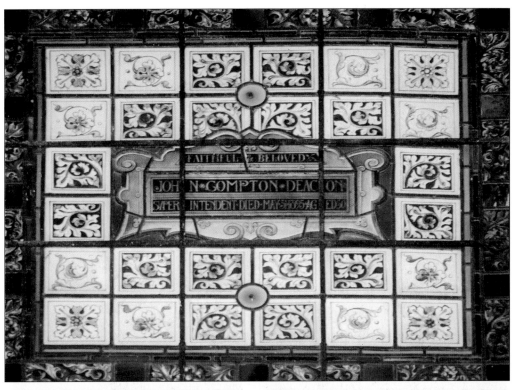

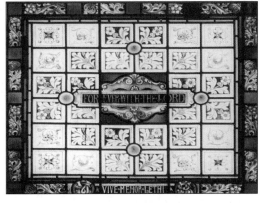

A series of eight windows, commemorating members of the congregation, designed and manufactured by Thomas William Camm of Birmingham, were placed in the chapel in 1900. Camm was also responsible for the east window in St. James, Wyesham and for the window depicting the Arthurian legend at Drybridge House (see p.118). After working with his brothers in the 1870s and winning a gold medal — the only one awarded to English exhibitors of stained glass — at the 1878 Paris Exhibition, he became the chief designer for the newly-formed stained glass department of R.W. Winfield & Co. of Smethwick. By the 1890s he was again operating his own studio, eventually with his children, Florence, Walter Herbert and Robert. Thomas died in 1912, but the firm continued to operate till 1967.

The Independent Congregational Chapel, Glendower Street

*Left: Seating of 1844 in the gallery of the chapel
with reversible backs*

*Below: T.W. Camm, who designed the commemorative panels in
the chapel, may also have been responsible for the four windows
in the library at The Hendre (below). They show
The Hendre, before and after Aston Webb added
the library, Llangattock church and
the Monnow bridge*

Other Monmouth chapels & churches

Top left: Kingdom Hall, once the coach house to 18 St. James Street
Top right: The Primitive Methodist Chapel in Monnow Street, designed by George Dobson
the pastor in 1863 when there were 220 members
Middle left: The Baptist Chapel in Monnow Street, now ruinous
Bottom left: The Kymin Church, built as a school c.1840
Bottom right: A board found under an upper floor at 35 St. James Square

Monmouth cemetery

After the parish churchyard had been condemned as 'crowded with putrescent mortality ... and the elements of incipient disease' the cemetery was opened on land bought from the Duke of Beaufort. The chapel (left) was designed by the Reverend M. Wyatt and built by C. Jackson in 1851.

Below is the base of the Paupers' Cross, unveiled on Palm Sunday 1911.

Monmouth School Chapel

The nave was completed in 1867 and the chapel was extended to include a library that became the chancel in 1875. The Shrine of Remembrance was opened in 1950.

Troy School Chapel

This chapel was built in the 1960s and has some good glass, made by Whitefriars Stained Glass Studios, which is set in concrete and lit from outside by floodlights. It was designed by K.W. Smithies of Bristol and built in 1964.

Brickwork

In 1614 the Haberdashers had to bring bricklayers from London to build the new almshouses and grammar school (p.67). But by 1860 there were at least three brickyards operating in Monmouth, one of them below the present School for Girls. Once the surplus stone from the dismantled County Gaol had been used, many substantial brick houses and terraces began to appear.

Top left: Westfield, The Parade, c.1870
Top right: Hall's Drapery, Monnow Street, 1883
Bottom left: South View, Dixton Road, 1893
Bottom right: Edgehill, Monk Street, c.1902

Brickwork

Top: Moat House
Left: Chapel House
Above: Cadogan House
All in Monk Street — the last flourish from the
Monmouth Brickworks (mid-19th century)

Brickwork

The Hendre (above) started as a shooting lodge built by G.V. Maddox for John Rolls about 1829. It was enlarged in 1833, 1837 and 1858, and about 1900 Sir Aston Webb added the library. The house contains a strange variety of doors, glass, carvings, panelling and ceilings.

The Rolls family were great benefactors providing Monmouth with the Rolls Hall, a gymnasium, a theatre, a Masonic Lodge, the Nelson Collection and large contributions to the hospital.

Above: The Union Workhouse, Monk Street
Right: HSBC building, Agincourt Square

Tiles — St. Mary's church

Tiles in St. Mary's church

When the parish church was rebuilt in 1732 many of the 14th- and 15th-century tiles remained beneath the new floor. They were found during the 1880 rebuild and placed on the walls of the tower. A selection of tiles from a house in Church Street, adjacent to the church gates, has been laid inside the south wall of the church.

Pugin became an enthusiast for church tiles and valued them 'near the head of those church ornaments which, next to stained glass, and when used in a whole-hearted way, must charm the eye'.

During the 19th century pseudo-medieval tiles became popular with firms such as Minton, Chamberlain, Wedgewood, Copeland and Godwin producing vast quantities.

Recent excavations have revealed that late 15th-century tiles were made in a kiln in Monk Street.

TILES

St. Mary's church

Above: 14th-century tiles from the Priory church
Below: Late 15th-century tiles also from the Priory church

(Drawings by Nicholas Molyneux)

Tiles — Monmouth School

Monmouth School Chapel contains mural tiles depicting the Resurrection and the Crucifixion. They were designed by Adam Kossowski and made by Otto Maciag and Michael Tovey in 1986.

TILES

Tiles — Evans Greengrocery

19th-century wall tiles in
Evans Greengrocery,
Monnow Street.

These large pictures, several feet high and composed
of many tiles, are almost unique in Monmouth.

Tiles — 19th century

Typical 19th-century flooring.

Monmouth Archaeological Society has revealed a kiln in Monk Street where many such tiles were made.

Top left: Caxtone, Hereford Road

Top right: Westfield, The Parade

Left: 21 Monk Street

Gateways

Top: Entry to the Burton Homes
Above: Wyaston Leys
Right: Monmouth School

The upper picture is taken from Chippenham. The Burton Homes were founded by Henry Burton and Mrs. S.E. Burton. The date on the gate is damaged but seems to be 21 August 1928.

Doorways

The obvious status symbol when building a house was the front door. The use of careful detail concentrated the gaze and along with the windows created the quality of the façade. The best example of the way in which the front door monopolises the façade is at Treowen (top left). Nothing so spectacular can be seen in Monmouth. Troy House has a fine flight of steps but an unimpressive door (left), whilst at Great Castle House it is the window over the door, rather than the door itself, to which the eye is drawn (above).

Doorways

*Far left: One of the great
doors leading to the
farmyard at Troy House
(parts are still in the stables)
Left: Troy House back door
(16th century)
Below right: The Robin Hood
(15th century)
Bottom left: south door &
Bottom right: west door
St. Mary's church
(19th century)*

Doorways

The average town house was not allowed to extend onto the street and had to be content, at most, with a small hood and fanlight. If the house was set back it could, during the Greek Revival, erect imposing porticoes, and Cornwall House, St. James House (top left) and The Grange did so. Other examples are at Oak House, Monk Street (top right); The Gatehouse, Monk Street (bottom left); and 16-18 Monk Street (bottom right). Many of the pillars supporting the pediment consist of three sections of wood enclosing a hollow centre filled with rubble; later ones make use of plaster.

Doorways

Top left: Chapel House
Top centre: Cadogan House
Top right: 18 Drybridge Street
Bottom left: 20 St. James Street
Bottom centre: 18 St. James Street
Bottom right: Royal George

Doorways & War Memorial

Castle View House (left) stands on the site of the castle gate and chapel and is of late 17th-century date. It acquired the fine shell-headed doorway in Queen Anne's reign. From 1810 until 1857 it was used as the Monmouth Dispensary. It has since been a military hospital, Conservative club and is now once again a private house.

The Catalapa tree was planted in the middle of St. James Square in *c*.1900. The War Memorial, by Reginald Harding, was unveiled in 1921. Cartref (alongside and below) became the dispensary in 1857.

Trellis porches

It was towards the end of the 19th century that a new form of porch was designed to replace the heaviness of the Greek Revival. This was the delicate trellis porch, both in wood and metal.

Top left: Singleton House, Monk Street (wood)
Top right: Wye Vale, Dixton Road (metal)
Bottom left: Lynwood, 14 Monk Street (wood)

Porches and Verandahs

Trellised porches became larger and larger until eventually the whole of the ground floor on one or more sides of the house was protected by a verandah. Most of Monmouth's verandahs date from the second half of the 19th century and were especially popular in the Dixton Road.

Top left: Porch at Ebberley House

Top right: Porch at 1 Wonastow Rd.

Left and opposite: Verandah at The Elms, Dixton Road — made of wood in a very similar design to the porch above

Verandahs

*Left & above: Trevethin,
Dixton Road (iron)*

*Above: Priory Lodge, Dixton Road (iron)
Left: The Elms, Dixton Road (wood)*

Verandahs

Top left & right: St. John's, Glendower Street (iron). It is on the garden side of the house and is illustrated in a catalogue from Coalbrookdale. Such items were sold by the yard and delivered with the castings fitted ready for fixing, and primed with a coat of paint

Above: 20 St. James Street. The posts and capitals are metal, the architrave wood with leaf decoration, and there is coloured glass in the centre circle

Left: Victoria Place, Priory Street. The greenhouse, with the verandah behind it, is dated to c.1840

Fanlights

Top and centre left: Newton Court. Internal fanlights lighting the back stairs and upper passages

Centre right: The Royal George

Lower right and left: Cornwall House

Fanlights

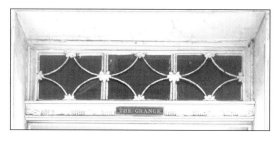

Top: Overmonnow House

Centre left: The Grange *Centre right: Oak House*
Bottom left: Priory Street *Bottom right: Priory Street*

Fanlights

Top: St. James Street

Centre left: Worcester Street
Bottom left: Priory Street

Centre right: St. James Street
Bottom right: St. James Street

Fanlights

Top left: Beaufort Court   Top right: 9 Agincourt Street
Left: St. James House   Bottom left: 22 Priory Street
Bottom right: Lloyds Bank

Doorways — Regency details

Doors and window frames usually have reed mouldings with lion heads and discs at the corners.

Top left & right, bottom left: Singleton House
Bottom right: Dixton, door to the conservatory c.1840

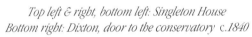

Windows

It has often been pointed out that the greatest contribution to human comfort was the introduction of glass into windows. Churches and grand houses had long enjoyed the luxury, but until the mid-16th century it was rare in humbler dwellings. To begin with, windows conformed to the usually low ceilings and tended to be horizontal. Throughout most of the 17th century they consisted of hinged casements with leaded glass.

Top left: Monmouth Priory c.1490   Top right: Dixton Cottage, taken from the church, 14th century
Middle left: 1 Agincourt Square, 17th century
Bottom left: Town lock-up   Bottom right: Troy House stables (demolished)

Windows — 3 Dixton Gate & Castle House

During the 1670s the sash window was imported from the Continent and was quickly adopted as essential to the proportions of a classical building. The windows were usually divided into 12 panes by thick glazing bars, and the boxing mechanism in which the frames were hung was flush with the façade.

Throughout the Georgian period glazing bars became thinner, windows became vertical rather than horizontal and with the introduction of the Window Tax in 1696 tended to become fewer. The tax applied to all houses with seven (and later six) windows. There are a few blocked windows in Monmouth, but with the repeal of the act in 1851 many were reopened.

Top right: No. 3 Dixton Gate, a burgage plot just within the gate
Top left & bottom: Great Castle House (1673)

Windows

Top left: King Henry V, Monnow Street

Top right: Sanroyd, Monk Street
(both Georgian)

Bottom left: Priory Street

Bottom centre: Shire Hall (1724)

Bottom right: Drybridge Terrace

The Gothic Revival came to Monmouth in the shape of the windows and the arrangement of the glazing bars. Dormers are rare before the 18th century, fanlights became fashionable at the beginning of the 19th, and stained glass was briefly popular at the beginning of the 20th.

Windows — Various

*Top left: Cornwall House
(1752)*

*Middle left: Chapel House
(c.1780)*

Right: 19 Agincourt Street

*Bottom left: The Royal George
(c.1800)*

*Bottom right: Monmouth
Hospital (1903)*

Decorative Glass

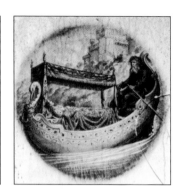

Drybridge House 1867

The legend of King Arthur in a series of upper lights
by T.W. Camm

Decorative Glass

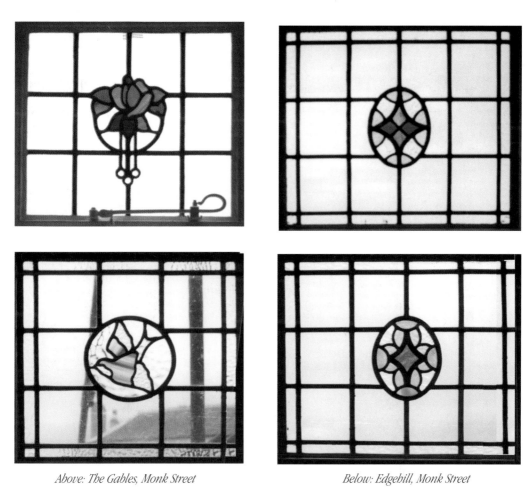

Above: The Gables, Monk Street   *Below: Edgehill, Monk Street*

Late 19th century

Fireplaces

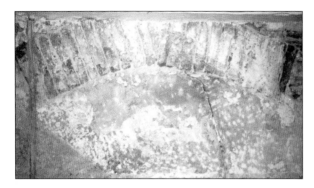

Second only to glass as a comforter, and for many centuries the principal means of keeping a house warm, is the fireplace. The old open hearth made upper floors impossible owing to the smoke, but by the end of the 15th century there are many examples in the Monmouth accounts of tenants acquiring small pieces of land, 3 feet wide, on which to build a chimney. These were built against an outside wall with an opening in the wall bottom for the fire. The oldest chimney in Monmouth is probably at the priory (above) and the oldest fireplace is in the Queen's Head (right). By the 17th century the fireplace had become the focal point of the room with decorated overmantels as at the King's Head and Great Castle House (below).

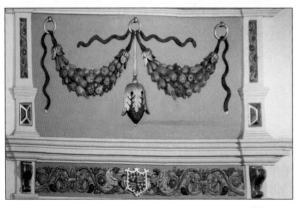

Above and left: The rather crude but lively
overmantel at the King's Head
Left: The elaborate overmantel of c.1675
at Great Castle House

Firebacks

The presence of fireplaces did not always meet with approval and the historian and topographer William Harrison wrote in 1587 in 'A Description of England' in *Holinshed's Chronicles* : 'Now we have many chimneys and yet our tenderlings complain of many rheums, cattarrhs and poses. Then we had none but reredoses and our heads did never ache'. Similar things have been said more recently about the introduction of central heating.

Top: 1668, Said to be the oldest example of the work of George White at Monmouth forge
The Forge continued to use charcoal until c.1812. In 1812 male labourers were paid 2s. 6d. a day
and females 1s. 6d. In 1831 it employed 80 people. (National Museum of Wales)

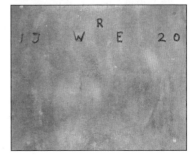

Middle right: 1642,
Sir George Probert,
The Argoed, Penallt

Bottom left: 1723, Found at Kingscot, The Parade

Bottom right: 1720, William Rea, Chapel House,
Ironmaster and Mayor

Fireplaces — Adam style

Towards the end of the 18th century the fashion in Monmouth changed to Adam-style surrounds, and many examples have survived.

This page:

Three fireplaces from North Parade House, c.1800

Opposite page:

Top left & right:
The Royal George

Middle left: Westfield

Middle right:
Chippenham House

Bottom left: Chapel House

Bottom right: Cornwall House

Adam style

Fireplaces

Top: Hilston Park, inserted c.1840
Left centre: Beaufort Arms
Bottom left: Great Castle House
Bottom right: Drybridge House

Tiled Fireplaces

Above: Drybridge House, 1867

Below: Cadogan House, Monk Street, 19th century

Victorian Fireplaces

Above and right: Caxtone, Hereford Road

Below: Trevethin, Dixton Road

Fireplaces — Various

Left: Slab for heating flat irons at Dixton Rectory
Above: Trivet or kettle stand, 20 St. James Street
Middle left: 9 Agincourt Street
Bottom left: 20 St James Street
Bottom right: 13 Whitecross Street

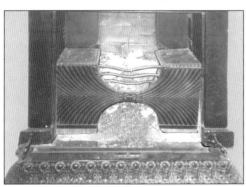

Stairways

There are stone spiral stairs at the castle (top left) of early 12th-century date, and in the parish church tower (14th century), while Treowen has one with wooden treads which may date from the 16th century (top right) and the building of the house.

Above: Priest's hole on landing at Treowen

Treowen also has a splendid well-stair of 1627 (left) setting a trend which was to make them the the main features of the larger houses of the gentry such as Troy House, Dingestow Court & Wyastone Leys.

Dingestow Court & Troy House

Top: Dingestow Court (late 17th century)
Bottom: Troy House (c.1673)

Stairways —Wyastone Leys

The fashion for well-stairs spread to the town and there are good examples at Chapel House, The Grange, Overmonnow House, Cornwall House, Chippenham House, The Royal George, The Gatehouse, Beaufort Court, North Parade House, Kingsley House, 15 St. James Street and The Chantry amongst others.

Wyastone Leys (this page) also had great influence on Monmouth fashion through the splendid series of concerts put on each year by professional musicians. It is now owned by Nimbus.

The house was rebuilt for J.M. Bannerman by William Burn in 1861.

Stairways — Various

*Top, right and left:
The Chantry,
Monk Street*

*Left: The Grange,
St. James Street*

*Right: Chapel
House,
Monk Street*

Well stairs

Top left: The Gatehouse

Top right: The Hollies (c.1750)

Above: Overmonnow House

Left: 20 St. James Street

Stairs — Dogleg & Geometric

Top left: Great Castle House introduced the dog-leg in 1673,
but it had few followers
Top right: Castle View (c.1690)   Bottom left: Shire Hall (back stair)
Bottom right: Beaufort Court (c.1770)

Stairs — Geometric

The most popular staircase in Monmouth, dating from the 18th century, was geometric with a continuous handrail enclosing an elliptical or circular area. Occasionally the doors on the landings of such staircases are curved as at Kingsley House and Beaufort Court. Elaborate iron balusters with stone treads were introduced in the 19th century into buildings like the Shire Hall, Rolls Hall, The Working Men's Institute and Priory Street School. Most Monmouth houses have good original staircases. They have survived because, whereas it is fairly easy to alter a fireplace, a window or a door, it is a major operation to replace a staircase.

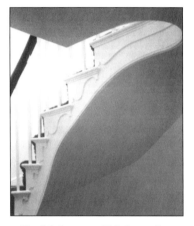

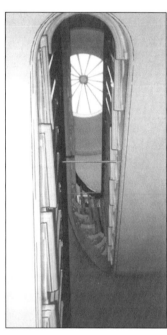

Top left & centre: 15 St. James Street
Top right: Kingsley House, Monk Street
Bottom left: North Parade House,
Monk Street
Bottom centre: Cornwall House,
Monnow Street
Bottom right: 30 St. Mary Street

Stairways — Various

Left: The Grange

Bottom left: Probably the best example of a continuous rail staircase is at Courtfield

Centre right: Parade House

Bottom right: St. John's, Glendower Street

Plasterwork

Once houses had lost their open hearths, ceilings could be inserted and craftsmen could then decorate them with plaster or paint. The earliest 17th-century examples in Monmouth seem to be the wall decoration at St. James House (*c.*1600) (top left) and the ceiling work at 1 Agincourt Square (top right). The most elaborate are those at Great Castle House (1673) (pp.137-38).

The ceilings at Treowen and Troy House (right and below) though roughly of the same period, are more restrained than those at Great Castle House. Once professionals had passed on their techniques to local craftsmen, lesser houses like Chapel House, and inns like The King's Head, began to decorate their ceilings and overmantels.

PLASTERWORK

Great Castle House, 1673

Great Castle House

Above: Ceiling details
Below: The ungainly infants are unfortunate and seem to be by a less experienced plasterer
than other parts of the ceiling (perhaps c.1700)

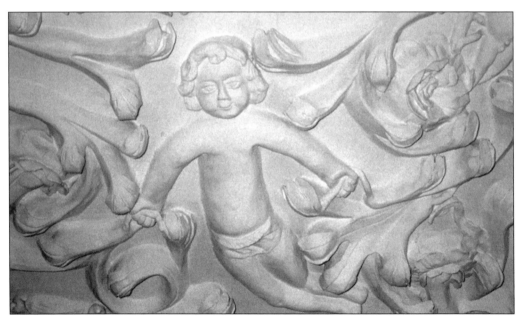

Roundels

The tradition of decorative ceilings was carried on into the 19th century in the pendents in Drybridge House (next page) and the roundels with which buildings like the Methodist church, the Working Men's Institute and the Rolls Hall surrounded their lamps and gaslights.

Top: King's Head   Centre left: Methodist church
Centre right, bottom right and left: Pentwyn (p.26)

Plasterwork — ceiling designs

Top left: Chapel House   Top right: The Gatehouse
Middle left: The Hendre   Middle right: The Queen's Head
Bottom left and right: The pendents in Drybridge House

PLASTERWORK

Plaster decoration

The Royal George

Although the house dates from
c.1735, the plaster decorations
inside and on the porch were introduced during a major restoration at
the beginning of the 19th century.

The lower illustration shows the
restoration of 1990.

The Picture House

**Triple Lantern Ltd
The Magic Lantern Theatre
Church Street, Monmouth, Gwent**

The Picture House, later the Magic Lantern Theatre, in Church Street occupies what has been called the oldest theatre site in Wales. The information on the following page is based on articles written by Michael Bartley and others.

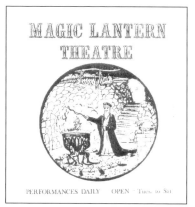

Assembly Rooms were built on the foundations of the Bell Inn by Thomas Penson in 1832. Ten years later he sold the building to the Oddfellows. In 1849 it was sold again and a year later the Bell Assembly Rooms became the Theatre Royal run by J.F. Rogers, but this enterprise only lasted for a year before closing.

The building took life again when it became the Corn Exchange, following which it was used as a roller skating rink for the nearby White Swan Hotel. It was not until 1910 that it was opened as 'The Rinkeries Living Picture Palace'. Two years later it was taken over by the Western Provincial Cinematographic Company who restored it and then sold it to the Perfect Motion Picture Company. Once again it was restored and renamed the Palace. After the First World War the entrance was moved to Church Street and it bore two new names — the Scala and the Regent. In 1927 the building was gutted and and reopened by Albany Ward as one of their Circuit Theatres named the New Picture House with seating for 600 and a stage. The first talking picture was shown in 1930, but the building closed in 1983 to reopen four years later as the Magic Lantern Theatre with seating for 450, and a skating rink at the rear. In 1989 it was listed Grade II by CADW. The building is now the Savoy, and a Trust has been set up to raise the £250,000 needed to restore it to its former splendour. Meanwhile it continues to show films regularly.

Plasterwork — The Picture House

The surviving decorative scheme dates from 1927 when the Albany Ward Circuit Theatres took the cinema over.

Top left: Base of the Proscenium Arch
Top right: Capital of the Proscenium Arch
Bottom Left: Details of plasterwork
Bottom right: Balcony bracket

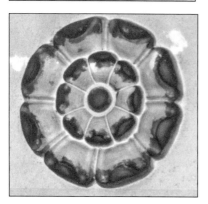

Panelling

Left: Troy House.

Some of the panelling was brought from Raglan Castle after the Civil War, most of which has since been removed to Badminton

Left: Dingestow Court. The drop-cresting at the top of the fireplace may have been part of a rood screen removed from a local church

Below left: Chapel House

Below right: Drybridge House

Ironwork

Monmouth forge operated from the early 17th century until the mid-19th and there were always numerous blacksmiths in the town. So most of the gates, railings, balconies and pillars were made locally. Objects such as the mace stand in the parish church were blacksmith-made, but the elaborate screen in the Lady Chapel was made by William Letheren of Cheltenham, and the Working Men's Institute employed a firm from Glasgow for its staircase.

Left: Troy House

The 18th-century iron gates at St. Mary's church (above and left) was a joint venture between the Parish and the Town Council.

In 1705 the Town Council ordered all its members and all innkeepers to put outside their door 'a good lanthorn with a sufficient candle therein lighted to burn' from 6 to 9 each evening from All Saints Day to the Purification.

Left: Cornwall House lamp-holder c.1770

Gates

The term 'iron' is often used to describe material which could be cast iron, wrought iron or mild steel. Usually a single iron object for a particular purpose would be wrought. A series of identical posts & rails may be cast iron bought from a catalogue. In the last 100 years mild steel has become readily available and has been used for the more expensive wrought iron.

Top left: Monmouth School

Top right: Chippenham

Left: Baptist Chapel

Ironwork

Top left: Edgehill

Top right: Westfield

Left: Wyastone Leys

Above: Working Men's Institute

IRONWORK

Gates & Balconies

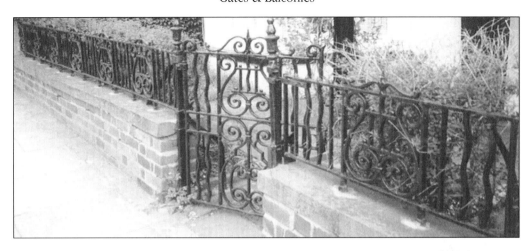

Top: Whitecross Street

Middle: 6 Agincourt Street

*Left: Beaufort Court
Balcony*

Ironwork

Above: The Congregational Chapel
Left: Capital of pillar supporting gallery made by Lawrence of Monmouth in 1851   *Right: Pulpit of 1844*

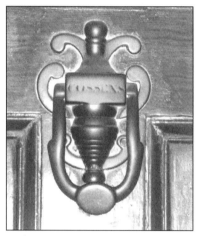

Centre: Mr. Cossens, the Postmaster for many years, had this knocker on his door in Church Street

Centre left: Drybridge House door plate

Centre right: The Mace stand in St. Mary's church

Bottom left: St. Mary's church. Screen of 1882 in the Lady Chapel

Ironwork

Top left: Monmouth cinema cash desk, 1927
Top right: Hilston Park shower bath
Bottom: Barrier protecting a corner of Beaufort Court,
possibly to prevent people committing nuisances.
There is another by Chapel House

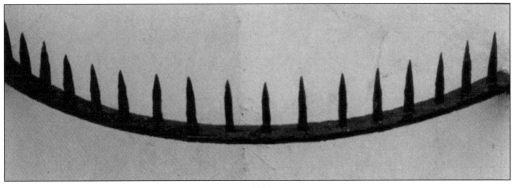

Memorials — Henry V and Charles Rolls

Henry V on the Shire Hall.

The monument was made by Charles Peart of Welsh Newton and erected in 1792 to attract men of taste who were doing the Wye Tour to visit Monmouth. Peart made portrait busts for Wedgewood, but this is not one of his better works.

Henry was probably born on 16 September 1387 rather than on 9 August.

Charles Rolls in Agincourt Square

Charles Rolls was killed in a flying accident at Bournemouth on 12 July 1910. The statue was made by Goscombe John and the plinth was designed by Aston Webb. Rolls is looking at a model of the plane in which he died, but the detail of the tail was destroyed when in a misguided attempt to clean the statue it was sand-blasted by the District Council.

Memorials

A far more regal portrayal of Henry V than the rather pathetic statue on the Shire Hall can be seen inside. Made recently by a group of local embroiderers, it shows the king encouraging his men as they go into battle. There is also an Agincourt Museum on the site of the battle in France.

Memorials & Oddities

THIS MONUMENT WAS ERECTED IN 1969 ON THE 25TH ANNIVERSARY OF THE BATTLE OF MONTE CASSINO TO COMMEMORATE POLISH SERVICEMEN WHO DIED IN THE CAMPAIGNS OF WORLD WAR TWO.

Monmouth has had a small Polish Community largely due to Cecil Cullingford who, as Headmaster of Monmouth School, employed Otto Maciag to teach art, Mr. Hardulak to teach music and Mr. Matterclas as boatman, along with his wife (above & left). The Cassino memorial is on the left bank of the Wye near Redbrook.

Bottom left: The White Swan Inn. Cupid on the swan's back. Lead, early 19th century

Below right: Drybridge House. Stone brackets supporting beams in the dining room ceiling, depicting animals and birds stalking their prey (1870)

MISCELLANEA

Wallpaper blocks

About 1890, Mr. Crompton-Roberts of Drybridge House decorated the houses in Drybridge Street with large wooden wallpaper blocks used for hand printing. He had a summer house made from them at his home and there were other buildings in Monmouth which acquired some. In Drybridge Street they have been painted over, but there are several in the Monmouth museum (bottom) in their original condition.

Miscellanea

Left: Firemark from St. Mary Street. One of six in Monmouth of which two are in situ, one on the Grange and the other on the Henry V.

Rain water heads

Right: Monmouth Hospital, 1903

Bottom right: Lloyds Bank, 1894, now the King's Head

Letter Boxes

Below left: Queen Victoria on the Hereford Road

Centre: Edward VII on the Parade

Miscellanea — Cupolas and Turrets

Top left & top centre: Shire Hall
Top right: Rolls Hall
Above left: Drybridge House
Centre: Union Workhouse
Bottom right: Beaufort Court

New Buildings

*Right and middle: New flats at Lancaster House,
Monk Street*

*Bottom: Woolworths use varying sizes of lettering
on their stores, but do not create
a pleasing façade*

MISCELLANEA

Somerset House, St. James Street

Above: Somerset House as a garage

Left: The Back of Somerset House

Below left: The Coach House

Below right: St. James Mews

Somerset House has good decorated ceilings, and has been at times the Labour in Vain Inn (with a sign of a blackamoor washing himself), the Judge's Lodgings, the Militia Officers Mess, a coach builder's workshop, and in 1926 a garage (above).

The recent development at Somerset House, where the old coach house has been replaced by St. James Mews (below), is welcome.

Caer Llan — The Berm House

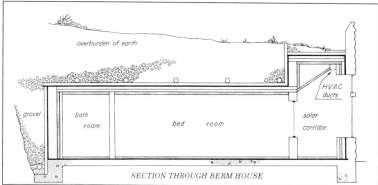

SECTION THROUGH BERM HOUSE

The shape of things to come. Caer Llan : The Berm House.

This was built by Peter Carpenter in 1988. It is an earth-sheltered house, receiving its energy from the sun, and is designed to be free of all space heating and maintenance costs for 500 years.

The building is designed to be 'massive' rather than 'lightweight' using concrete blocks and stone in considerable quantities giving both structural and thermal stability. Although this represents greater capital outlay than a conventionally built house, it does provide three cost saving advantages:

1. Its life expectancy is much greater than a conventional house spreading the capital costs over hundreds rather than tens of years.
2. The choice of materials cuts maintenance costs to negligible amounts in the forseeable future
3. The great thermal stability, coupled with other features, helps to eliminate all space heating costs completely.

Index